Strange Wind from the Roanoke

By

Maxville Burt Williams

This book is a work of fiction. Places, events, and situations in this story are purely fictional. Any resemblance to actual persons, living or dead, is coincidental.

© 2003 by Maxville Burt Williams. All rights reserved.

No part of this book may be reproduced, stored in a retrieval system, or transmitted by any means, electronic, mechanical, photocopying, recording, or otherwise, without written permission from the author.

ISBN: 1-4107-6546-6 (e-book)
ISBN: 1-4107-6545-8 (Paperback)

This book is printed on acid free paper.

1stBooks – rev. 09/02/03

ACKNOWLEDGEMENTS

Thanks to Mrs. Mebane Holloman Burgwyn and Mrs. Jackie Allsbrook for their suggestions and critical review of this novel. I also would like to thank my wife, Mary Lois, for her support and encouragement.

FOREWORD

STRANGE WIND FROM THE ROANOKE is both fact and fiction. It is fact in the sense that it follows the great effort that William R. Davie put forth to get the United States Constitution ratified by the people of North Carolina.

Although some of the characters in the novel were real people the story of Sam Pickett is fictional. I have first and foremost attempted to write an historical novel about the life of a young man who is trying to find some meaning to his life.

To that end this novel was written.

Other books by Maxville Burt Williams are FIRST FOR FREEDOM, REFLECTIONS, THE SCHROONCHERS AND THE SCHROONCHERS MEET THE FLIM FLAM MAN.

Chapter 1

The silent snow fell and gently settled on all the trees, roads and houses until the entire town of Halifax and the surrounding countryside were blanketed with an ermine coat. Sam Pickett stood by the window and looked from William R. Davie's law office and could not recall when there had been such an accumulation of snow in such a short time. This January of 1787 would be one to remember. King Street, the main avenue, was beneath at least two inches of snow, and the flakes seemed to be getting larger even as he watched from the window. Limbs and branches of trees were already laced with a spectral beauty. The small fireplace crackled with spitting sparks that flew up the chimney. To Sam, this was a sure sign that bad weather was "setting in". That's the expression Sam remembered when he thought about the way older people referred to weather that was to be long and dreary.

Sam had not been feeling well all day and now wondered how long his employer, William R. Davie, would be in Warrenton. Business would be slow until the snow was gone and the roads could be traveled again.

From the window he could see three young boys scampering along the street, throwing snowballs at a passing sleigh being driven by a young man who was accompanied by his lady friend. The two lovers were sharing the same blanket and were sitting closer than was necessary to keep warm. As he watched the passing scene, he caught his reflection in the window pane and his attention was captured for a moment by what he saw—a young gentleman with dark brown eyes and heavy eyebrows, a firm nose, and a gentle lingering smile of empathy as he thought of the young lovers. Sam studied his reflection—the cheek bone perhaps a little high, the chin a bit too strong, but he was pleased with the thick finely-chiseled lips and the dark hair, which was tied at the back with a ribbon. The reflection was suddenly lost from his vision as he noticed the familiar figure of Reverend Ford coming down King Street. The lanky man in dark clothes had turned up the top of his coat collar. A large black felt hat was pulled down over his ears. The Reverend looked up toward Sam as he turned off King Street to the undisturbed snow-covered walkway that led to the law office.

Sam moved from the window to the door and opened it before the minister had time to knock.

"Afternoon, Sam. I wanted to catch you before you closed for the day. I'm glad to see you're still here." The Reverend took off his hat and shook the snowflakes from it.

"This weather is not fit for man nor beast. Come to the fire," invited Sam.

Reverend Ford took off his overcoat and threw it across a large high-backed chair and went immediately to the fireplace. After briskly rubbing his hands together before the fire, he turned to Sam.

"I'm not here on church business, Sam. I've come to bring you a letter that came addressed to me yesterday, I don't quite know what I should do about it and I thought you needed to be aware of its contents. It's from your father-in-law, John Hamilton."

The Reverend turned away to his heavy coat and took the letter from the inside pocket.

"Does Christopher Dudley know about the letter?" Sam knew that Dudley was known to open almost everybody's mail. Since the tavern served as the Post Office, Dudley was the first to see the incoming mail.

"You're the first one who has seen it other than myself. Not even Dudley opens my mail. I have given him strict orders that he is not to meddle in the affairs of the church, and to this day he has honored my command."

Reverend Ford handed the letter to Sam.

Sam looked at the postmark. "I see it was mailed from Boston two weeks ago. It's signed HIS MAJESTY'S CONSUL OF MASSACHUSETTS."

"I noticed how it is signed. He's still in the service of the King," acknowledged the Reverend.

Sam cast a surreptitious look at the minister. "You'd think that he's a member of the royal family. I've never seen such loyalty."

"He was the same way about the church. He was one of the greatest contributors in my congregation before the Revolution. I could always depend on his faithful support. You know, no one has occupied his pew since he was made to leave Halifax."

"I suppose people find it hard to forgive a man such as he," said Sam.

The Reverend held his coat before the fireplace to warm it as Sam silently read the letter.

The contents made Sam reflect about those experiences in Hamilton's past—old and bitter times—how he was so despised because of his loyalties to the crown— and—how change had come so violently to this small town.

The letter was a sincere request to visit Halifax. John Hamilton seemed to want some assurance that his coming would not cause any dissension. He asked about the mood of the people and requested information about the owners of the property that had been taken from him by the Council of Safety back in 1776. Sam thought about how long ago that had been. He counted the years in his mind and said out loud. "He wants his land back. Twelve years have passed and now he wants to come back to Halifax."

"Sam, I hope I haven't put any burden on you by bringing you this letter," said the Reverend.

Sam looked up as he folded the letter. "I'm glad you came by, Sir. I just don't know what to do about it."

"Perhaps Davie can give you some advice. He's always abreast of this sort of thing."

"I'll speak to him about it when he returns. He's still in Warrenton."

"Looks as if he might be there for a while. I think this snow is just beginning," said the Reverend, glancing toward the window.

"I had a letter from him yesterday. The trial is over, but he's staying on for two more days on some other business."

"I meant to ask you about that trial. You know, I'm always interested in my flock. Montfort and McCullen are two of my most generous contributors. I hope Mr. Davie presented an able defense. We'll have to live here among these people. I never did understand the circumstances under which they were brought to trial. I've just heard enough about the case to be completely confused. What did the court decide about Henry Monfort and Benjamin McCullen?"

"Well, it seems the military commissioners: McCullen, Montfort, and John Macon of Warren county, issued some certificates for money to soldiers who were not supposed to be compensated. The charges were that some certificates were issued to men who had no military service at all, and that some soldiers received money that were not deserving." Sam spoke in a matter of fact manner since he was not aware of all the details.

"Were the certificates cashed by the State Treasurer?" The Reverend seemed to be getting a little too persistent.

"That's my understanding. However, I don't know all the facts. Mr. Davie only wrote to me about the verdict."

"And what was that?"

"Macon and Montfort were acquitted and McCullen was fined two hundred pounds and given a sentence of twelve months in jail. He is to serve his time here in Halifax."

"We'll have to see to his comfort, Sam."

"This is the worst time of the year to be confined to that damp jail. McCullen is liable to catch his death in that place," said Sam.

Reverend Ford nodded sadly.

"Give my regards to Mr. Davie when he returns, and let me know if I may be of further assistance to you, Sam." The Reverend struggled into his heavy overcoat.

"Thank you for coming out on a day like this, Reverend."

"Sam, you keep the letter and do with it what you want. I just hope that Hamilton has the good sense to stay away from Halifax. There are many that have not forgotten him. If he does decide to come back, he should be made aware of the feelings of the people here. Some of them still don't think the war is over."

Strange Wind from the Roanoke

Sam followed the minister to the door. "I'll certainly make him aware of the mood of the people in Halifax. He would be taking a great risk, if he should decide to come back here now."

After cautioning the Reverend about his footing along the steps, Sam closed the door. He walked to the fireplace and fed the struggling flames a fresh log. He thought of the trials that had taken place throughout the state when other Tories had tried to regain property that had been confiscated during the war. —None had been successful.

He moved to the front window and considered the bitter attitude that still prevailed in Halifax. Tories had not been forgiven and John Hamilton led the list of those Loyalists who were the most hated.

It had been six years since the defeat of Cornwallis, and four years since the signing of the Treaty of Paris that officially ended the American Revolution. Yet, the signing of a treaty did not insure safety and forgiveness to those Tories who had fought for the Crown. Even though Hamilton was his father-in-law, this letter was the first communication that he had received since the war had run its course.

As he held the letter before the light at the window, Sam recalled how John Hamilton had fought so bravely in Georgia—how he had led the Loyalist troops against the Colonials.

How could this man even consider coming back to Halifax? Sam thought how concerned Josie had been about her own acceptance in Halifax when she returned after the war. Now, Josie had been dead for over five years and her father had not visited her grave—not even once.

Sam folded the letter and placed it in the top drawer of his small desk. He decided he would leave it there until he had time to think about just what he would write to Mr. Hamilton.

He took his coat from a coat rack near the desk, slipped his arms into the sleeves, placed a screen in front of the fireplace and left the office.

Walking from the office, Sam was careful to place his boots in the footprints that had been left by the Reverend Ford. With each crunching sound, he had to stretch his stride to follow in the prints. How different had been the steps taken by John Hamilton. The strides he made during the war had all led in the wrong direction.

When Sam came to King Street, he lost the footprints of Reverend Ford, for now they had become mingled among many shapes of parallel trails that had been made by passing sleighs and tracks of horse-drawn wagons and carriages.

It had been Sam's habit to visit the cemetery at least once a week since Josie's death and even though the snow was falling fast, he turned off King Street for his routine visit. The cemetery was just across the road from the law office and Sam could see the stone that marked Josie's resting-place whenever he stood at the office window.

Now he made his way among the stones until he found that special plot of earth. The snow had covered the slab of marble and Sam knelt to brush away all that had accumulated. Words began to appear beneath the snow and Sam's lips moved as he read to himself:

JOSIE H. PICKETT
1760-1783
TREAD GENTLY ON THIS HALLOWED GROUND
THE SOUL OF MY LOVE RESTS BENEATH THIS MOUND

Sam took the last letter that Josie had written from inside his coat pocket, as he often did when he came to the grave and read it through, word by word. He had almost worn the letter out but he had always folded it with care when he placed back inside the envelope.

Reading the letter somehow made him feel closer to Josie. The snowflakes fell about him as he unfolded the letter.

To my Beloved Husband,
I am writing this with a weak hand and hope you can follow my thoughts. The last few days have been painful, and my mind at times seems to fade just when I have a clear thought. I know of your love for me, and you can have no doubt of how I care for you —not only for the present or the past, but for all the future that will be yours. I feel sad knowing that I shall not share the future with you, and that maybe I have not been long enough with you to tell you what great hopes I have for you. The greatest comfort that I could take with me is knowing that you will find happiness, although I shall not share it with you. You are young and the future is

before you. I can only be thankful for the time we have shared and hope that as the years pass—our time together will continue to be remembered as a special time that will last forever. Although my days with you seem so brief, they have been filled with all the happiness and joy that could come from the union of a man and a woman. I am aware that there will be others who will want to claim your time, and I am sure you will find happiness for your future years. I want this for you. You deserve a better life, for you have had so little happiness. If you could but grant me one last wish, it would be your promise to marry again and find meaning and purpose to a life that is just beginning to find its place in time. My love, I shall take with me to the grave and hope that when you pass my resting-place you will consider that beneath this earth—there is a soul who wants only happiness for you. God bless you for your endearing devotion that shall sustain me forever.
Your Love
Josie

Memories are tricky phantoms that are conjured up to satisfy a longing for the past.

Forgotten feelings are called back—perhaps to escape the pain of the present. Misty recollections become clear when viewed with thoughts of times long since past. Thoughts lengthen during these pensive times to dwell on sweet moments. In his recollections, Sam thought how strange it was that time could be so short when he had wanted it to last forever—and then how it could linger and linger when he wished it away. Now, as he thought of time and fate, it seemed that these companions had schemed and planned a cruel and unmerciful act on his beloved Josie and left him with little hope for the future.

Sam recalled the good times of his childhood, when he and Josie's brother, George Hamilton, had to tolerate Josie's presence. Then, there were those days of happy love when he finally saw Josie grow up to be a beautiful young lady. Sam felt that he had never realized how much he had loved Josie until the war came and she had to leave Halifax with her Loyalist family. Josie would have been arrested along with the rest of her family if they had chosen to stay in

Halifax after the Revolution had begun. When the war came to an end, Josie had returned to Halifax. Then came their hasty marriage and the six months they had spent together in Edenton while he was completing his apprenticeship under a master surveyor.

That time was a special time in his life—those months of love and happiness were the most glorious days he could remember. They were both so child-like in their devotion to each other. Each day, when he would return to the rented cottage, was as if he had been away at war and the two had not seen each other for years. At night they would pretend that they were back in Halifax and were proud parents of a son and a daughter. Oh, how they had planned—children—a farm—nothing was beyond their wildest imaginings.

There was a tender smile on Sam's face as he remembered the happy times spent at Edenton. The smile faded and Sam could feel the tears coming to his eyes. Josie was frail and weak on the day of their marriage, but Sam felt that time would heal all the old wounds that had lingered after the war. Because of her weakness, she had perhaps been more susceptible to illness. Upon their arrival, Sam was alarmed when he heard that there were cases of smallpox in Edenton. They were there five months when Sam learned that Josie had been taken to the quarantine house at the edge of town. In panic-stricken haste, Sam had hurried to the house, which was used as a hospital. Only those who had previously contracted the disease were allowed to tend the sick and Sam was refused admittance. He was told that there were seven victims there, and only two were expected to live. An attendant, Jeremiah Sledge, had brought the news of Josie's death and the special letter. The last letter of Josie's was a part of Sam's life. He kept it on his person from the day he received it. The only other item that Sam was allowed to keep was Josie's brown leather-bound journal. It had been her habit to write about experiences and private feeling that she shared with no one, not even Sam. Once she had promised Sam that he would be allowed to read it when the time was right.

Some weeks after the funeral, Sam took out the journal and began reading the flourishing script of his beloved wife. He became so engrossed with the passages that he could not put it down until he had read the entire journal. Some entries were about her family, some were about her friends, and those special times he had spent with her. There were poems and expressions of devotion that Sam felt were personal. These were the pages that he frequently turned to at night before he retired. Somehow it made him feel closer to her and sleep would come to him and perhaps bring dreams of those happy times.

Now, standing by Josie's grave, Sam looked at the letter. It was written with a weak hand, and the words seemed to tremble even as Sam's hand trembled. It was so unlike Josie's script of earlier days—times before her illness. If only he had the power to reshape those troubled times in his past—then, the present would be so different. Sam realized that his thoughts were now dwelling too much with fate. He felt he had been a victim of that strange and unpredictable word.

Gently, Sam folded the letter and put it back inside the worn envelope. There was a wetness on his cheeks as he slowly moved away from the grave. Carefully stepping among the stones, he made his way back to King Street. He walked across the street and turned right onto Market Street. To his right was the Halifax Courthouse, then Martin's Tavern was just beyond the Courthouse and on the same side of Market Street. All along the street were shops and stores, and at the end of Market Street on Sam's left was the most popular place in Halifax—Dudley's Tavern.

Sam looked toward the tavern and the snow continued to fall. The snow was getting lighter and Sam could see that at least two inches had accumulated. He thought this wonder must be one of nature's most beautiful sights, but, without Josie, the quiet beauty of the blue-white scene was lost in the emptiness of his loss. Sam had no real appreciation for anything without Josie. The very fact that she could not share this beauty—made it all seem meaningless. Though Sam appreciated nature's way of showing its splendor, he did not feel that the beauty touched him—for he was beyond any depth of such feelings. Perhaps, beauty to others who passed along the street held a meaning quite different from the impression that he felt. He was simply indifferent to all the beauty that nature had so lavished upon the quiet town.

As he came down Market Street he looked to his left and saw a shadowy silhouette of Looney Oney scratching and plundering in the trash behind Dudley's Tavern. Willie Jones had brought Looney Oney to Halifax when he moved into "Grove House". She was known to conjure up concoctions to cure rashes, snake bites, fevers and she could talk the devil out of people who were possessed by that evil spirit. People in Halifax speculated about Looney Oney. Some said she was a witch. Slaves thought of her as a doctor. Then, there were those who thought of her as just plain crazy. Those who thought of her this way had given her the name "Looney Oney".

Sam stepped up to the snow-covered walk in front of Dudley's Tavern and walked inside. As he entered the tavern, he saw the round-bellied Dudley at the end of the bar. He was a jolly fellow, about fifty, with a thick growth of hair on his chin. The rest of his face was cleanly shaven. His bulging eyes and snubbed nose cause him to look almost comical. His happy disposition made him a most agreeable tavern-keeper.

Sam walked quickly to the counter.

"Hey, Dudley! Have you got anything hot? It's cold outside."

"You know I've got whatever people need. How about some hot chocolate?"

"Sounds like a good idea."

"Sam, I was beginning to think that I was gonna be my best customer."

Dudley handed Sam a mug of chocolate and came from behind the counter.

"Come over here by the fire."

Sam followed Dudley. "I want to talk to you, Dudley. I've got something that I don't know how to handle."

"Well, you know me, Sam. I'll do what I can."

Sam and Dudley sat close by the fireplace. When they were settled, Sam looked quickly into the concerned eyes of his closest friend.

"Dudley, I just read a letter from John Hamilton. It seems he wants to come back to Halifax. He thinks he may be able to get some of his property back that was taken by the Council of Safety."

"Well, he won't be welcomed here. He, above all others, should know that. That property has changed owners several times since 'Seventy-Six'. Is this the first time you've heard from him?" There was a look of distrust on Dudley's face.

"I didn't even know if he was dead or alive until I read that letter." Sam sounded almost apologetic.

Suddenly the back door was flung open and in with a cold draft of air came Jesse Turner who was struggling with Looney Oney. The old swamp woman tried to pull free as two of Jesse's cronies followed closely behind, laughing and enjoying the fun.

Strange Wind from the Roanoke

Sam looked closely at the ragged homespun coat and the black felt hat that had lost its shape. The hat covered her ears but was pushed back on her head to reveal two muddy looking eyes arched with heavy brows. A long pointed nose dominated her face and made it appear to be triangular. Long silky black hair hung about her rounded shoulders. She was unlike any other person Sam had ever known. The characteristics were so mixed in her that she did not belong to any given class or race of people. Sam could not see into her past any more than he could see beyond her cloudy eyes. She was, without a doubt, the most enigmatic person Sam had ever known. One thing was certain with Sam and that was he'd rather have her as a friend than to risk being her enemy.

"Look-a-here, Dudley. Look what I found scratching in the garbage barrel out back of the tavern." Jesse Turner seemed pleased that he had apprehended the thief.

His beady eyes looked intently at his companions. Turner had long arms that seemed to be loosely attached to his shoulders. Sam had often thought how Jesse's face resembled a possum's face. He was tall and had a long pointed nose. Dudley had once remarked that Jesse could do what no other man in Halifax could do and that was to overlook that big, long pointed nose.

"Let me be, Jesse Turner. Oney ain't done you no harm." Oney tried again to get free from Turner's grasp.

"Seems like you ain't too choosey about the company you keep, Jesse," yelled one of the cronies sitting near the fireplace.

"You know what I told her when I saw her picking up them scraps?" His arms were now firm as he held his prey.

"What did you tell her, Jesse." One of the men came to Jesse's rescue.

"I told her to git inside and eat. You ain't no better than nobody else."

All the men joined in the laughter.

Dudley stepped forward and walked toward Jesse and said, "Jesse Turner you beat all I've ever seen. I told Oney she could have them scraps from the kitchen. I put the food out there for her. Now you let go of her." There was a threat in his voice and Jesse immediately turned her loose.

"Jest having a little fun wid her, Dudley. Jest having a little fun," said Jesse as he backed away from Dudley.

Oney gathered her burlap bag and started toward the back door. When she got to the door, she turned to Jesse Turner. "One day you'll be sorry. One day shame will come to you. Oney ain't to be treated this way."

"Excuse me, Miss Oney. I must of thought that you were somebody else," said Jesse, pretending to apologize.

As Oney left the tavern, she turned to Jesse. "The shame you put on me will come back to haunt you. When you suffer in your shame, you'll remember me. SHAME—SHAME —Jesse Turner".

"Let her be, Jesse," warned Dudley. "You just let her be."

"I need to be gittin' on home. Ooo—oo—ooo, I hope that Looney Oney ain't out there waiting for me," said Jesse, pretending to be scared, as he looked back with a lugubrious expression on his pointed face.

"Jesse Turner enjoys making people look like fools," said Sam.

"He'll get what's coming to him one of these days," assured Dudley as he walked with Sam to the front door. Dudley reiterated his feelings about John Hamilton. He assured Sam that Hamilton would be taking a great risk if he chose to return to Halifax for any reason.

The temperature had risen several degrees but Sam felt a slight chill so he pulled his coat collar up closer around his neck as he left the tavern. The snow was not as heavy and the flakes seemed to be getting smaller. Just as he stepped down from the porch of Dudley's Tavern, he saw three young boys running from behind the courthouse toward Looney Oney. Snowballs were being thrown at Oney who stood as if she dared the boys to come closer. "You boys stay away from me," shouted Oney.

"What are you doing in town in broad open day? Witches don't come out 'til it gets dark," yelled the oldest and biggest boy.

The other boys began to shout in unison as they circled Oney. —"Boney—scrawny—Looney—Oney—Boney—scrawny—Looney —Oney.

Sam quickened his footsteps. "You boys stop that. What do you think you're doing?"

When the boys saw Sam, they quickly ran behind the courthouse. Perhaps to wait for another prey, thought Sam as he approached Oney. "You won't be bothered anymore, Oney."

Strange Wind from the Roanoke

"Thank you, Mr. Pickett. Dem boys didn't mean no harm—dey jist boys—but Jesse Turner —he's a grown man. He will haft to answer for his deeds. Shame will be on him." Sam could tell by the look in Oney's eyes that this was no idle threat.

Sam walked along the street with Oney and learned that she had come to Halifax to help Mrs. Eelbeck with the candlemaking. Whenever she came to town, she was "put up" by Mrs. Eelbeck in a room with a fireplace just off from the kitchen. She usually spent two days making candles. Oney had her own beeswax, and she could make the colors and aromas of the candles better than anyone. Oney told Sam that she got her honeycombs from "Uncle Louie" the stablemaster on Willie Jones' plantation. When "Uncle Louie" finished extracting the honey from his twelve beehives he kept all the honeycombs for Oney. Oney wanted Sam to know that beeswax made the best candles.

"People don't know how easy it is. All you do is boil the honeycombs in water and let the wax rise to the top. Then you jist dip it off. When it gits hard, you jist melt it agin and strain it. What takes so long is the dipping. The real secret is how to git the right odor when the candle burns. Now dats why my candles are so good, and Oney keeps what she knows to herself."

Sam also was informed that Mrs. Eelbeck had told Looney Oney to stop by the tavern. Dudley had left word for her to stop by whenever she came to town. Sam was better satisfied that Oney would not have to try to get back to her cabin in the swamp. If the weather didn't clear up, Oney would have to spend more than two days in Halifax.

Sam had found a certain comfort in his friendship with Mrs. Eelbeck. The room at the boarding house was all a young surveyor needed. He had never cared much for accumulating furniture and the like—he even felt a certain satisfaction just knowing that Mrs. Eelbeck and her servants would tend the room.

The boarding house was the last house at the corner of King and Pittsylvania. As Sam turned to go up the walkway, he was breathing as if he had run the last mile. Oney continued to the back of the house where she was to work her magic with the candles. Sam suddenly realized that he was completely exhausted. While he was hanging his coat on the coat rack next to the front door, Mrs. Eelbeck came from the kitchen.

"Sam, you're going to catch your death if you don't stay out of this weather," said Mrs. Eelbeck, as she wiped her hands on her apron. It was her habit to do that. Sam had noticed that she would wipe her hands with her apron even when it was not necessary. Sam thought that perhaps it made her more comfortable or it made her appear to have just finished doing something important.

"You know, I felt a chill just as I left Dudley's Tavern."

Mrs. Eelbeck came closer and put her hand on Sam's neck. "You're beginning to fever, Sam. You'd better get to bed."

Mrs. Eelbeck took Sam's arm and led him to the stairs.

Sam was astounded by the strength of Mrs. Eelbeck's arm as she supported him. She was a robust woman, but as gentle and kind as any woman he had ever met. Her wide mouth and large brown eyes were always smiling. She was the most approachable woman in Halifax. There were no strangers known to her.

When they came to the top of the stairs, Mrs. Eelbeck and Sam stopped just in front of Sam's room.

"You go on and get in bed. I'll be back with a foot warmer."

Mrs. Eelbeck turned left and went immediately down the hall to get Jessica Jackson.

It was only a short while after he had gotten into bed that he heard Jessica and Mrs. Eelbeck outside his open door.

"You stay with him. I'll send for Dr. Joyner," said Mrs. Eelbeck. Sam was vaguely conscious, but he was aware of the deep concern in Mrs. Eelbeck's voice.

"But he's out of town. I heard he went to Northampton County around noon," said Jessica.

Mrs. Eelbeck turned back toward Jessica to speak as she went to the stairway. "Well, we'll have to do what we can to help him through his chill. I'll fetch the warmer for his feet. You stay with him."

Jessica waited momentarily then she gently knocked on the door. When she entered the room, Sam was beneath a patchwork quilt and the chill had now caused him to shake. The bed seemed to vibrate and Jessica went to the wash basin and dipped a towel in some water.

"Why Sam, you're burning up with fever." She placed the wet towel on his forehead.

"It came so suddenly. I've been feeling bad all day—but this chill just took me by surprise."

Strange Wind from the Roanoke

"I hear there is much sickness hereabouts. Doctor Joyner was called to Northampton. I fear the snow will not permit him to return until sometime tomorrow."

"I'm so weak. If I should get through this—it will have to be because of someone else's strength."

As Sam's fever rose, his eyes became dazed and soon his mind began to fade from the present to a time in his past when he had been sent out by General Allen Jones to determine the whereabouts of Cornwallis' Army. Vivid recollections of the scouting assignment now occupied his mind. It was May of 1781, and Jessica was with her mother at Sadie's Ordinary. Sam begged both Sadie and Jessica to come with him to Halifax to seek refuge from the coming army of Cornwallis. After a very convincing argument by Sadie Jackson, Sam gave in and left them both to face the coming army. Sadie Jackson later died as a result of the bizarre acts of several British soldiers. Jessica, being young and strong, survived the ordeal and had decided to come to live in Halifax when the war was over. Sadie's Ordinary was sold and Jessica bought a shop and then moved in with Mrs. Eelbeck.

Jessica was a beautiful young lady with blond hair and a trim figure. The feature that Sam thought most attractive was her eyes. How like Josie's pale, blue eyes were they. Although there were similarities between Jessica and Josie, they were only slight. The differences were more pronounced. Jessica had always been a hard-working girl, and what she had now come to possess was because of the labor and effort that she had shared with her mother. Josie, on the other hand, had never had to work. Her mother, Abigail Hamilton, was always certain that Josie would marry well and would never have to want for anything.

Suddenly, Sam sat up. "Josie, Josie, I need you. Help me Josie. Oh, Jessica, it's you. I'm so cold. I need something to keep me warm."

Jessica spoke softly to Sam and he relaxed and closed his eyes. His thoughts were now of Jessica.

When Jessica moved to Halifax, she took all the money she had acquired from the sale of Sadie's Ordinary and filled her shop with goods such as: cloth, leather, candles and various and sundry items that were needed by the people of Halifax. Much of the business that had been John Hamilton's before the war now became Jessica

Jackson's trade. Bits and pieces of information—unrelated facts—scattered thoughts were darting at a hectic pace in and out of his consciousness.

Mrs. Eelbeck entered the room. She had the foot-warmer wrapped in a thick, blue cloth, and went immediately to the foot of the bed and placed it beneath the cover next to Sam's feet.

"He's been shaking with the chills since I entered the room," said Jessica.

"Oney is making candles she just may have some idea about what we can do. We must do all we can to break the fever," said Mrs. Eelbeck as she tucked the covers closer to Sam's body.

Suddenly Sam sat up and flung the covers from the bed. "The British will be here by noon tomorrow, General Jones. I'm cold, General—where's Josie—I need Josie." His eyes looked straight ahead and his eyelids did not flicker.

"He's delirious. We need to bring the fever under control." Mrs. Eelbeck picked up the cover from the floor.

Jessica tried to calm Sam and gently encouraged him to lie down. "What can we do?"

"When I was younger, I struggled with Mr. Eelbeck for an entire night. I held him close in my arms and used my body to keep him warm and calm. He swore to his death that I kept him alive. It's the only way I know to help. I'm going downstairs now to tell the other boarders to keep quiet. You'll have the upstairs to yourself, and I'll see that you are not disturbed. You stay with him. He probably will think you're Josie, that should make it easier for you to help him."

"Are you suggesting that I use my body to keep him quiet?"

"You do what you must. I have only told you what I know. If you decide that it will be necessary, you'll be the only one who will ever know—unless you want to tell me."

"I'll do whatever I need to do," said Jessica, with resolute determination.

"The fever should run its course by morning. We'll know more then. I'll send for Dr. Joyner tomorrow—if he's back in town."

"Well, I suppose it's up to us, Mrs. Eelbeck."

"It's up to you, Jessica. I'll be downstairs if you feel that you need me." She stepped softly to the door and gently closed it behind her.

"We need more gunpowder, General. The soldiers are beginning to leave camp," said Sam. Again he sat up and threw the covers to the floor. Jessica hurried to gather the blankets and placed them on the bed.

Jessica took her coat and draped it over the chair next to the bed, moved the candle from the bedside table and placed it on the small table near the door; walked quietly back to the bed and slipped in beside Sam. She held him close and spoke softly. Several times he tried to sit up, but his weakened body was held as Jessica struggled to hold him close to her. He soon was calm.

Sam responded to her tender touch and reached out to her.

"Josie, Oh, Josie. It's been such a long time since I've held you like this."

The small candle near the door burned out and room was dark.

****

It was close to daybreak when Jessica quietly slipped out of bed. Her dress was damp from the perspiration that had come from Sam's fevered body. She reached down to touch his clammy forehead and felt sure the fever had broken. He was no longer hot and the perspiration had stopped.

Sam's eyes began to flicker as the early morning light filtered into the room. He saw or thought he saw an apparition moving slowly and quietly toward the door. Was the figure real or a ghost that was playing with his senses? Was she a part of his past or was she the one who had brought comfort to him during the night? He closed his eyes and tried to gather what scattered bits of reality he could remember.

Chapter Two

Sam Pickett was sick for ten days. During the time of his illness, the widow Eelbeck and Jessica Jackson gave him the best of care. Oney had sent him a candle with a special aroma that Oney claimed was most effective when bad spirits were about. During this critical time, his feeling for the two ladies developed into a deep affection. He thought of Looney Oney as one of the reasons for his recovery. The aroma from the candle filled the room. He tried to identify the source of the odor and finally decided that it was a secret known only to Oney. How Oney captured the fragrance was beyond Sam's understanding.

His days were pleasant enough, but he dreaded the nights for he knew what would come with sleep.

The most disturbing phenomenon that plagued Sam's sleep was the ever-recurring dream of Josie's funeral. The dream had been a part of his life since that fateful day. It was always the same. As often as three times a week the dream would return to haunt him. It always began with the docking of the sloop bringing Josie's body back to Halifax. At Willie Jones' wharf stood phantoms of faceless men and women dressed in black against a white background of snow. So vivid was each detail, as the body was taken from the boat to be placed on a black-fringed carriage. When the procession began its ascent to the river road, the horse pulling the carriage with Josie's body slipped along the incline and fell lame. All the black figures stood motionless except a single rider who slowly dismounted and methodically hitched his horse to the carriage. Soon the procession began to move again at a lifeless pace until it arrived at the cemetery.

This vision had been a constant reminder of what Sam knew to be the saddest day of his life.

Sam was so disturbed by the dream that he felt he needed to tell someone about it. He had the opportunity to talk at some length about his dream to Christopher Dudley when he came by for a visit. Dudley was one person to whom Sam felt he could confide his most secret thoughts. When He told Dudley how the dream continued to haunt him, Dudley suggested that Sam talk with Looney Oney.

"Now there are people who think the old swamp woman is a nuisance and should not be allowed in town. You know, like Jesse Turner."

"What do you think, Dudley?"

"Sam, I'm telling you—Oney has the gift. She can see through things that other people don't even know are there."

"How about dreams? Can she tell you what they mean?"

"She can do it, Sam. I'm telling you. She's done it for me. Sometimes I catch her scratching around in my trash out behind the tavern and I slip her some scraps and a little wine. Then, when I ask her about certain signs or omens, she tells me what they mean. Sometimes she says things that are hard for me to understand. She's got the gift, Sam. No doubt in my mind—she's got the gift."

Dudley was so convincing that Sam promised himself to seek Oney's advice whenever the opportunity presented itself.

While Sam was confined to his room, word reached him that William R. Davie had returned to Halifax and had been appointed by the North Carolina Assembly to serve as a delegate to the Constitutional Convention in Philadelphia. Davie had been by the boarding house and had left word that the office was to be kept closed until Mrs. Eelbeck had given him word that Sam was well enough to return to work. Davie did not venture to come close to Sam's door for fear of contracting the contagion.

There was news that Willie Jones had also received an appointment to serve as a delegate to the Constitutional Convention that was being held in Philadelphia, but had refused the appointment. When Sam heard the news, he wondered just what reason Mr. Jones had given the Assembly for his refusal. Then, after he had considered Willie Jones' nature, he assumed that whatever the reason was—it must have been a good one and perhaps should not be questioned.

Several months had passed since Sam's illness. While at work, Sam often thought about the Revolution. Since the birth of the nation, the infant had been in its formative years and was now struggling to find some foundation for its future.

When news of the victory of Yorktown had reached Halifax back in October of 1781, there was a wild celebration that lasted for several days. Freedom became an omnibus word and people throughout the land used the meaning that best satisfied their conscience or their way of thinking. From Yorktown, came-trailing celebrations ignited by the strong flame of freedom, which came to towns, large and small, throughout the land. The great rejoicing of the people would die down in one place like a smoldering ember only to flare up in another place at a later time. When the wind of change swept across the land, the celebrations in other places were as wild and as exciting as the one Sam had experienced in Halifax.

Sam recalled how he felt the night the news reached Halifax. With all the chaos and disorder that had come with the news, he had wondered if freedom would destroy the hopes and dreams of the brave men and women who had struggled through the Revolution. Freedom had not only brought independence; it had also brought fear. The feeling that had so excited the people had to be tamed like some wild beast before there was freedom for anybody. These last five years had been a period of taming and the spirit of the people was now well in harness. As wild as it was back in 1781—it was a time that was his to cling to for the rest of his life—a time to be remembered that would live far beyond his short existence in the scheme of things.

Now in the summer of 1787, men were being called to Philadelphia to consider what kind of government was needed for the new nation. Sam felt that the nation was ready to stand alone and if men were courageous enough, perhaps the time would soon come when the United States would be strong enough to take its first step. Maybe—with the proper instructions and the seasoned wisdom of the delegates—the childlike nation would soon hold its place among the

Strange Wind from the Roanoke

more mature nations that already stood upright with their heads held high. Sam thought that much could be learned from the experiences that the people had endured during the Revolution. With prudence and common sense, the thinking of the people could be molded to create a government that would be at least as good as the ones that would be imitated. Since this was a new nation, there would be ample time for the delegates to consider what system would best serve all the people.

Sam kept up with all that was happening when he assumed his duties at William R. Davie's law office. From the beginning, when he had taken the job as Davie's personal office attendant, Sam had continued to do work for those who needed land surveyed. Since he had been educated to be a surveyor, Sam had made an agreement with Davie that he would work at the office from Monday through Thursday and leave Friday and Saturday to catch up on his surveying. This had been a most agreeable understanding with Davie since Sam had only been interested in law for the past two years and was not yet convinced he wanted this profession to be his life's work.

William R. Davie had been in Philadelphia attending the Constitutional Convention for two weeks and it was the twenty-seventh of September before Sam received any word from his employer. Davie had requested that all his mail was to be forwarded to his new address, and he mentioned that the delegates had been sworn to secrecy. This being the case, there was little he could mention of the proceedings of the Convention. Since there was so much to consider, it was quickly determined that the delegates must first agree among themselves before the issues were debated among the people.

While Sam was tending the office, he had much time to think about all the changes that were now taking place. There seemed to be two ways of thinking that prevailed throughout the province of North Carolina and throughout the country. One political group felt that the country needed a stronger national government—while those who opposed this philosophy felt that a confederation of states would best serve the interests of the people. These two opposing philosophies could be recognized even in Halifax. William R. Davie and his father-in-law, Allen Jones, were strong for a more powerful national government—while Willie Jones led those who felt that the states should retain the power and the national government should exist at the pleasure of the states. Sam fancied that the pains of labor had come during the great revolution and when the birth of the nation was finally realized, it was as if the infant nation was now trying to stand alone.

There was a postscript to Davie's letter that caused Sam's mind to return to his own obligations to Davie. He read these lines again and out loud: SEE TO THE COMFORT OF BENJAMIN MCCULLEN. GO BY THE JAIL AND TELL HIM OF MY CONCERN FOR HIS WELL BEING.

Sam reflected about the trial that had taken place in Warrenton and felt strongly that Benjamin McCullen was no more guilty than the others for issuing false documents to the soldiers. After all, those certificates required three signatures before the treasurer could cash them.

Sam sifted through Davie's mail and had addressed those letters he thought demanded Davie's attention, and was now ready to take them to Dudley's Tavern to be posted.

After locking the front door to the office, Sam turned down King Street and immediately noticed Jessica Jackson standing alone in the cemetery. He stopped and watched her for a moment, then walked across King Street to the entrance of the cemetery.

Jessica's back was turned toward him when he came to the place where she stood. He looked down and saw the headstone of Sadie Jackson and could see that Jessica had brought some fresh flowers and had placed them in a small vase just against the stone.

Standing almost close enough to touch her, Sam could smell the captivating aroma of lilac that always seemed a part of her presence. Sam spoke softly. "We both have much to remember from our past, Jessica."

"Oh, Sam, you came so quietly."

"I saw you standing here just as I left the office."

"I like to bring flowers here as often as I can. Mother loved flowers."

"They're beautiful. I'd like to get some for Josie."

Sam turned toward Josie's grave as he spoke and saw a vase of red roses on the mound. He looked at Jessica.

"You brought roses for Josie, too."

"Well, I really picked more than I needed. Mrs. Eelbeck suggested that this would be a good place for them."

"You two are getting to be my keepers."

"Sam, everybody needs somebody. That's just the way life was meant to be, I suppose. I put some on your mother's grave and your Aunt Jenny's, too."

"Your thoughtfulness for my loved ones is more than I expected."

"You've had so little time to do anything since your illness. I just wanted to be of some help."

Sam looked into the pale blue eyes of Jessica. "You do know that I appreciate what you've done. Thank you, Jessica."

For a tender moment Jessica looked into Sam's eyes and there was something about her look that held more meaning than all the words that had been spoken by either of them.

Suddenly the moment was gone and Jessica turned from Sam. "Well, I must be getting back to the shop. It's almost time to close. Good-bye, Sam."

"Good-bye, Jessica."

Jessica walked from the cemetery and Sam watched her until she was beyond his vision. He then walked to his father's grave and looked down at the stone. His father's resting-place was on the right side of his mother's grave. The stone was older but it had weathered the changes over the years. Sam did not remember too much about his father. He was only seven years old when his father died. Now, as he looked at the stone on the other side of his mother's grave, he felt a certain comfort just knowing that his Aunt Jenny was resting there. He thought about how his mother had struggled to make a life for them during his early boyhood and how tenderly she had cared for Aunt Jenny. She was, in death, much the same as she had been in life—close to his mother Sarah Pickett.

Sam carefully stepped away from his mother's grave and stood for a moment at the precious spot where Josie rested. He did not take the letter from his pocket, as he had done so many time in the past, but the words from Josie's last letter now echoed in the recesses of his mind—IF YOU COULD BUT GRANT ME ONE LAST WISH, IT WOULD BE YOUR PROMISE TO MARRY AGAIN AND FIND MEANING AND PURPOSE TO A LIFE THAT IS JUST BEGINNING TO FIND ITS PLACE IN TIME.

Sam looked at the sun and realized that it was time for the afternoon stage, so he hurried from the cemetery.

Upon entering Dudley's Tavern, Sam was surprised to see such a large crowd of men. Jesse Turner was standing with his lanky body resting against the counter. It was evident to Sam that Jesse had been drinking most of the afternoon, for his eyes were glassy and he was somewhat unsteady as he used the counter for support. His face was flushed and beady eyes seemed to look in the direction that his nose was pointed. He had a way of finding bad in anything, and seemed to overlook the good in everything. Turner had a following at Dudley's Tavern, and there were always those few cronies who nodded approval to whatever subjects Jesse took as his text.

Sam nudged his agile body to the counter and found an empty stool next to Jesse.

"All of us here fought for our freedom and now it looks like the delegates in Philadelphia are going to turn this country into some kind of tyranny." Jesse's words were loud enough for all the men to hear.

"What makes you say that, Jesse?" Dudley became aware of what Jesse was saying. Sam sensed that this was the first time Dudley had expressed any interest.

"Well, I've heard talk that the Convention in Philadelphia is being held behind closed doors. We won't even know what they're talking about until all has been said and done."

Sam could never understand where Jesse Turner got his information. Somehow he managed to know more than people gave him credit. Sam handed Dudley several letters and Dudley turned his back to place them in the out-going mailbox.

"I just had a letter from Mr. Davie yesterday, and he said that the delegates need time to get some understanding of the issues before they are put before the public for debate." Sam hoped his explanation would satisfy Turner.

"I'd like to know where everybody stands on the issues. How are we supposed to know if it's all done in secrecy?"

There was a rumble of support from Jesse's supporters even before he had completed the sentence.

Sam stood up and faced Jesse squarely.

"Jesse, everybody here knows how much you gave to the cause. The delegates, as I understand it, are trying to get some plan of government for us to follow. Our freedom won't mean much of

Strange Wind from the Roanoke

anything unless we have some kind of trust in our delegates. What we need is some law and order."

Jesse again looked at the men sitting to his left. "I just hope we don't end up worse than what we were before the war."

Sam looked beyond Jesse Turner and could see Mr. Allen Jones coming from the game room. He was dressed in a dark brown waistcoat and light brown knee britches. His white shirt had ruffles at the wrist and around the neck. He was a most distinguished looking gentleman. Here was a man who was respected by all the people in Halifax. "Mount Gallant", his plantation in Northampton County was his pride and joy. However he spent much of his time in Halifax. He had the great honor of being one of the members of the committee to write the "Halifax Resolves". He was educated in England and was one of the most influential people in Eastern North Carolina. His great dedication to the townspeople during the war was something that people still talked about whenever General Allen Jones' name was mentioned. He had taken complete charge of the evacuation of the town when Cornwallis and the British had descended upon the town back in 1781. Allen Jones had also been Sam's benefactor. He had paid the expenses at Edenton when Sam had studied to be become a surveyor. Mr. Jones had also been instrumental in getting employment with William R. Davie. This was not too hard for Allen Jones since William R. Davie was his son-in-law.

There was a serious look on Mr. Jones' face and his dark eyes registered concern, as he walked to the counter.

"Still fighting the war, huh, Jesse?" Allen asked the questions as if he already knew the answer.

"I just don't know what the country's coming to, that's all."

"The men meeting in Philadelphia will do what they think is best for the country. Why don't we leave it to them to come up with some plan of government," suggested Allen Jones.

Dudley leaned across the counter. "I understand your brother Willie is not too interested in what's going on in Philadelphia. Have you talked with him lately?"

"Willie, even though he is my brother, does not always share my thinking, nor I his."

"I hear he's against any kind of government that will overrule the states and take away the freedom of the people," Jesse seemed eager to add some information.

"Well, Willie has good reasons to feel the way he feels. I, myself, feel we can solve some of the problems he's so concerned about after we have some kind of national government with enough authority to act," explained Allen Jones.

Jesse Turner looked as if he could not find enough room in the tavern to continue with his lecture so he turned and almost fell when he started for the door. "I'm going to the common and tell everybody I see what this country's coming to. We're in worse shape than we were before we ever fought the British. Come on fellows, I can't just stand out there and talk to mah self."

"You'd better go somewhere. I'm getting tired of your mouth," said Dudley.

Several cronies meandered toward the door. Just as they were leaving, a small red-faced man ran wildly into the tavern.

"Harry Bedlow is down at his blacksmith shop just as drunk as a skunk. I just saw Sheriff Whitehead and six men on their way to arrest him," said the sanguine messenger.

Allen Jones turned to Sam. "You know, that Bedlow is a good a man as ever lived, but when he's drinking he's like a wild beast."

"It'll take at least six men to bring him under control," said the messenger. "I understand he's already tore up his house before he came to the shop."

"How about his wife? Is she alright?" asked Sam.

"The last time I saw her she was running towards the stage coach with a bundle under her arm yelling at the top of her voice. — I'VE HAD ALL I CAN TAKE—I'M GOING BACK TO EDENTON TO MY FOLKS! WHEN HE SOBERS UP, YOU ALL CAN TELL HIM WHERE HE CAN GO! I can't say that I blame her for leaving town. I'd hate to be around a two-hundred and fifty pound man like Harry Bedlow when he's drunk and out of his mind."

With these words, the man turned and left the tavern. Sam looked intently at Allen Jones. "You know, Sir, there's a lot of truth in what Jesse was saying a while ago."

"I agree with you, Sam. I'd never let Jesse Turner know it, though. What we'll just have to do is wait and see what happens in Philadelphia. There are some capable men attending that Convention. I have faith that what is decided there will give us the framework that is needed to form a government. From all I can understand about it,

Strange Wind from the Roanoke

the states will have to give some kind of approval to whatever action is taken there. I think even Willie would approve of that."

"Like you say, we'll just have to wait. There's not much else we can do until the Convention makes some kind of decision."

"I left John Ashe at backgammon to come out here to see about all the loud talk. I'd better get back and finish our game. Let me know when you hear some word from Davie."

"I will, Sir."

Sam turned to leave and threw up his hand to Dudley as he walked out the front door. He had decided earlier in the afternoon that he would stop by the jail and speak with Benjamin McCullen before he returned to the Boarding House. As he walked to the corner of Market and King, he wondered what had happened to Jesse Turner and his cronies. The common was deserted except for old man Hedgepeth who sat on the wooden bench at the corner. Coming to the town common in the late afternoon was Mr. Hedgepeth's daily ritual. He called it his social hour. Here he could strike up a conversation with old friends and catch up on the latest news.

"You been sitting here very long, Mr. Hedgepeth?" Sam looked at the old man's kind but wizened face.

"Been here long enough to see Jesse Turner git arrested," said the old man.

"What Happened?"

"Well, Jesse got too loud. Sheriff Whitehead heard the shouting and came from the blacksmith shop to see what Jesse was yelling about. When Jesse accused him of being a Tory-lover, the sheriff took him to the jail."

"What happened to all his cronies?"

"Seems they didn't want no part of spending the night in jail, so they went their way when they saw the sheriff coming."

"Jesse was riled up when he left Dudley's. Maybe now he'll sleep it off." Sam seemed better satisfied now that Jesse was where he needed to be.

"I don't know about that. When Sheriff Whitehead took Jesse to the jail, them six men came dragging Harry Bedlow from the blacksmith shop. They had him bound in plowlines and he was still raving like some kinda wild man. Won't hardly a stitch of clothes on him when they took him to the jail. I speck, he's about the strongest man I've ever seen."

"Well, I'd better go on over there. I need to see about Benjamin McCullen."

"Bob Whitehead don't never lock the front door—so I speck you can just walk right in—if you've a mind to. I speck it'll be kinda crowded. Ain't but two cells and there's three of 'em."

Sam thanked Mr. Hedgepeth for the information and continued toward the jail.

As he walked along King Street, he thought to himself that Halifax did not need a "town crier". Mr. Hedgepeth was no crier but he could tell you all the news. It was always good to see him on the common. He was a part of all that made Halifax a special place.

When he turned to go to the jail, Sam saw Reverend Ford coming from Mrs. Eelbeck's Boarding House.

"Hold up there, Sam," yelled the Reverend, hurrying his pace.

Sam waited a moment and Reverend Ford came closer.

"Just wanted to remind you, Sam—the church social—starts at four o'clock tomorrow at the common. We'll auction off all the ladies' food baskets. Now, you know we need the money for the new sanctuary. All the ladies are trying to out-do each other this year. We should have some fine food—all donated—mind you."

"I see you've been down to sample Mrs. Eelbeck's goodies."

"Just happened to be in the neighborhood. We couldn't have a social without her. Her basket always brings more than any other. See you tomorrow, Sam."

"I'll be there, Reverend."

As he approached the front door to the jail, Sam was conscious of complete silence. Not a sound was coming from inside the brick structure.

Inside the jail there was a desk and a chair at the center of the large room. Two rough chairs were to the left of the desk and a wooden bench was to the right. Just behind the large chair, which was Sheriff Whitehead's seat, were two small cells. In the cell to Sam's right was Benjamin McCullen, who motioned for Sam to come closer. He held his finger perpendicular to his lips, indicating that Sam was to come quietly.

There was a stifling odor that permeated the room. Both cells had an inside toilet, which was a platform about three feet high and about three feet square with a small rounded hole, which was the source of the repugnant odor. "The Throne", as this structure was

Strange Wind from the Roanoke

called, served no king. A sliding curtain could be pulled to give whoever was using the throne some privacy.

Sam looked quickly to the other cell and could see Jesse Turner squatted in the far-left corner opposite the bunk where Harry Bedlow lay snoring. Jesse looked terrified sitting next to the "Throne" with only his underwear to cover his body. Jesse returned Sam's stare, but did not speak.

McCullen came quietly to the front of the cell. His bearded face and long hair told of his six months' confinement. McCullen looked to be in good health.

"I just came by to see about your needs. Mr. Davie asked me to check on you from time to time," said Sam, in a whisper only loud enough for McCullen to hear.

"I'm fine, Sam. Jesse Turner is the one somebody needs to be concerned about." McCullen motioned as he looked toward the adjacent cell.

"What happened to his clothes?"

"Just as soon as the sheriff left, Harry Bedlow made Jesse Turner take off all his clothes—and lo and behold—he found a knife in Jesse's pocket. Harry told Jesse he was going to kill him with his own knife when he woke up—that is—if he's still in here."

"So that's why Jesse is being so quiet," said Sam, now understanding why the squatted figure of Jesse Turner looked so rigid.

"Jesse didn't want to give Harry his clothes at first, but when Harry slammed him up against the wall a few times—well—Jesse started taking off his clothes quicker than you and me together could skin a rabbit."

Sam looked at the sprawled figure of Harry Bedlow on the bunk. Jesse's pants only covered his thighs therefore the top was not buttoned. Jesse's shirt was not large enough for Bedlow's broad chest, and he looked funny in the clothes that were only half-large enough for him. The huge man was in a deep sleep and his snoring and snorting were louder than any words that had been spoken.

Jesse glanced imploringly at Sam and tiptoed to the front of the cell. He did not take his eyes off Harry Bedlow as he moved forward. With his hands cupped in front of his red underwear, Jesse looked like the devil walking on a bed of hot coals.

Sam moved to the front of Jesse's cell, and as he did, Harry Bedlow gave out a loud snort. Both Sam and Jesse stood frozen in their places. Then, Harry seemed to be more comfortable and continued in his deep sleep. Sam moved closer to Jesse.

"Sam, you've got to get me out here. That crazy Bedlow is going to kill me when he wakes up."

"I'll fetch the sheriff. You stay quiet. He should release you when he comes back. You look sober enough now."

"Oh, I'm sober as a judge. Tell him to hurry—and—ah—Sam—Sam—don't slam the door when you leave and tell Sheriff Whitehead to come back here as fast as he can—and tell him to be quiet when he gits back here."

Sam stepped softly to the front door and was soon on his way to Mrs. Eelbeck's Boarding House.

He found Sheriff Whitehead at Mrs. Eelbeck's table and told him Jesse's urgent request. Several men at the table stopped eating long enough to hear Sam's story.

After gathering some clothes for Jesse, Sam returned to the dining room and handed the bundle to Mr. Whitehead. Sam had always thought of Whitehead as a good sheriff but he would take his time about his duties. He was a short, stocky man about fifty years of age with red hair above his ears but none on top of head. Sam told him how anxious Jesse was to be released, but the Sheriff made no effort to hurry himself.

"It would serve him right to let him stay in there for the next two days," said Sheriff Whitehead, as he pushed his chair back from the table. "I'll go see about him. Got so a man can't eat his meals in peace no more. It's like this all the time. I need to find myself some other kind of work. I'm getting too old to have to put up with other people's troubles all the time."

Just as the sheriff was leaving the table, Mrs. Eelbeck brought a bowl of stew from the kitchen. "Take this to McCullen. Jesse and Harry don't need to be given no special attention. If those two could taste this stew, they would probably want to stay there forever just so they could get some more."

Sam sat down at the place that had been vacated by Bob Whitehead, and Mrs. Eelbeck brought him a bowl of stew. Everybody seemed eager to hear more about Jesse Turner's predicament, but Sam thought it would be better if they were to hear it from Jesse himself.

As Sam began eating his supper, he thought about old man Hedgepeth sitting at the town common. It would be quite a while

Strange Wind from the Roanoke

before the old man would witness as much as he had seen this afternoon. There was no doubt in Sam's mind that the story would take many shapes with the tellings that would come from the old man—and how about Jesse Turner—what kind of story would Jesse make of the awkward predicament that he experienced. Sam smiled to himself as he thought of Jesse Turner's point of view.

Then he thought of Looney Oney's promise to Jesse when he had made so much fun of her at the tavern—SHAME—SHAME—SHAME.

Chapter 3

It was twilight when Sam finished his meal. He complimented Mrs. Eelbeck for the fine supper, then excused himself. He went immediately to the front porch and settled in one of the large green, wooden rockers, just to the left of the front door. He watched the shadows fall across King Street and wondered about the shadows that had fallen across his life these past five years.

Since Josie's death, there had been so little appreciation of anything that had once seemed important to him. He quickly tried to call back all those things he had loved in the past. The town, the surrounding countryside, and the people all held treasured memories of sights, sounds and events that would linger in his mind as long as he had the memory to call back those times: The glow of sunset, — summer nights—chasing fireflies with his boyhood companion, George Hamilton—strolling through the town and knowing all the people he met along the way—the sound of crickets—when darkness fell. Places like Martin's Livery, just down King Street, where Market Street joined the main avenue; where the odor of manure made all who passed the livery stables aware that they were doing a thriving business. Then, there was Market Street, where people came to display their goods, wares, vegetables or whatever they had to sell on

Market Day. Some of Sam's happiest memories were of the times he spent in town on Saturday.

There were two special places on Market Street. One was the Courthouse, where the first official act for independence was formulated by the Fourth Provincial Congress back in April of 1776, and the other was Dudley's Tavern, where perhaps as many decisions were made by the delegates as were made at the formal meetings inside the Courthouse. And—around all of this flowed the Roanoke River. When the rains were heavy, there was an occasional flooding and the banks could not hold back the swollen river. It was that way when Cornwallis and the British Redcoats had descended upon Halifax in 1781.

There were good memories of his early boyhood on the Randolph Fleming Farm. Here he had spent his youth. There were fond reflections of his mother's strength and the sweet, fresh scent of the new earth being prepared for planting; the pungent odor of dried tobacco being packed in hogsheads; the smell that floats from the smokehouse on hot summer nights. There were so many bits and pieces of life that now darted among his reflections. Halifax was the place where he first realized that his love for Josie Hamilton would completely change his outlook on life and his very being. A smile came with these special thoughts about his serendipitous youth.

Suddenly it occurred to Sam that if the past five years were sad, — then it was because he thought they were. Could it be the way he had looked at life? —- Could it be that life was not altogether the way he had viewed it from his particular point of view? Sam remembered he had read somewhere that someone once said WHAT YOU SEE SOMETIMES DEPENDS ON HOW YOU LOOK AT IT. Maybe—just maybe—it was time for him to consider the present and the future and let the past rest in its proper place. Now he was mature enough to understand that life did not always offer happiness to all—especially those who did not seek it. Perhaps he could find some purpose for his future. He was still young enough to at least make a sincere effort. This thought fascinated him, and sitting there in the growing darkness he decided to consider it more thoroughly in the days to come.

Sam's thoughts were abruptly interrupted as the front door opened.

Maxville Burt Williams

"Sam, that's the eatingest bunch of men I've ever tried to feed. I actually think I'm losing money at this boarding house" said Mrs. Eelbeck, stepping in front of Sam and sitting in the rocker next to him.

"Maybe you should cut back on you helpings." Sam stood, as Mrs. Eelbeck sat down.

"Oh, I like to see hungry men eat all they want. What-cha-doing sitting out here by yourself?"

"I enjoy this time of day. I've just been thinking."

"I've been meaning to have a talk with you, Sam."

"You have?' Sam looked intently at Mrs. Eelbeck.

"Yes, and maybe now is as good a time as any," Mrs. Eelbeck nodded as she rocked.

"You know, it may just be a coincidence, but I've been wanting to talk to someone. It's just I can't seem to find the right time."

"Maybe you need to find the right person, too, Sam."

"I was just wondering a while ago, Mrs. Eelbeck—do you think it's possible that I'll ever forget all that's happened to me?"

"Why should you forget, Sam? You shouldn't —but then again; you can't let your past become your present. You have to look at the past for what it's worth. You can't relive it."

"It's hard to forget—especially —Josie."

"I felt the same way about Henry Eelbeck. I still remember the good times. You know, Sam it is not often we find someone we love who loves us just as much."

"It was that way with Josie and me."

"There is no greater feeling than to LOVE AND BE LOVED. It is a joy that gives meaning to our lives. When we have such a relationship, we can count ourselves among the fortunate ones who are BLEST.

"It will be hard to find someone to take Josie's place."

"Now we're getting somewhere. That's exactly what I wanted to talk to you about, Sam. I know no one can take her place with you. That's your problem. You must realize that no one wants to take her place. If some young lady is interested in you, then she'll want to make her own place—not take someone else's place."

"I suppose I've let the past be too much with me."

"Time has a way of getting things sorted out, but sometimes it needs to be given a nudge here and there."

"I'm glad you came out here, Mrs. Eelbeck. You make me feel better about what I am going to do."

"And just what is that—if I'm not being too bold?"

"I'm thinking about asking Jessica to go with me to the church social at the town common tomorrow afternoon. What do you think about that?"

"It's not so much what I think as what Jessica thinks. But, I think I already know what she thinks."

"Do you think she'll go?"

"Jessica and I have been cooking most of the day in preparation for the social. She's not about to stay away. Fact is, she told Reverend Ford how much she was looking forward to it. He was by earlier."

"Did he sample your pastries?"

"Like he always does. He just kept nibbling away. I finally wrapped up some gingerbread in a cloth. Then I ran him out of my kitchen. Otherwise, I don't think we'd have enough for tomorrow."

"He told me that he just happened to be in the neighborhood."

"He always just happens to be in the neighborhood when I'm cooking up for a church social. There's still much that needs doing—so let me get back to my kitchen."

Sam stood and pushed his chair back to make more room for Mrs. Eelbeck to pass. "Will you ask Jessica if she'll come out here for a while?'

Mrs. Eelbeck acknowledged Sam's request by nodding and giving him a flirting wink. Several times during their conversation Sam felt that he wanted to tell her about the disturbing dream of Josie's funeral—but decided that he did not know quite where to begin. Now, he put this thought aside and concentrated and even practiced what he would say when Jessica came to the front porch.

He hardly had time to get his thoughts organized before Jessica was standing in the doorway. Sam rose from his chair immediately.

"Mrs. Eelbeck said you wanted to talk to me, Sam." Said Jessica as she walked past Sam.

"Come and sit down for a while. You—you know, I'm not a religious man, Jessica. I don't attend church as often as I should—but

I do think the church social tomorrow is going to be a good thing and I can see the need of money for building a new sanctuary. What I want to do is help in any way I can. So, I thought if you were going and if I were going—then perhaps we could attend the social together." Jessica sat down.

"Do you feel that it's your Christian duty to take me to the social?" admonished Jessica.

"Now, Jessica," Sam squirmed uncomfortably. "You know I didn't mean for it to sound like that."

"Well, you sounded like you were ready to start building the sanctuary yourself—and you wanted me to be your helper."

"Let me begin again, Jessica?" He leaned forward. "Tomorrow there's going to be a church social at the town common. It would greatly please me if you would allow me to escort you to the common. Will you honor me with the pleasure of your company?" Sam asked the question as if he were play-acting.

"I'd like that, Sam. Your invitation is most graciously accepted. Thank you," said Jessica, joining the act.

"Tomorrow is Market Day, so we should have a large crowd."

"I think the Reverend planned it that way," suggested Jessica.

"I've never bought a lady's basket before—suppose I end up getting a married lady's basket?"

"You don't have to worry about that. All the married ladies will have their husbands with them. Their names will be called out each time a basket is up for auction. No one but the husband will dare bid on it. The Reverend knows what to do. This is not his first auction."

"How will I know which basket is yours?"

"Mine will have a large red ribbon on it. You can't miss it, Sam."

Jessica extended her hand to Sam as she stood. "Now, I must see if there is anything I can do in the kitchen to help Mrs. Eelbeck. I'm sure she'll want to know what we've been talking about."

"We should leave here around four, don't you think?" Sam released her hand and as she walked by him he caught a wisp of that lilac aroma.

"That sounds good, I'll see you then." That aroma faded as Jessica walked away.

Sam stayed on the porch for a while and then went up to his room. He stepped lightly about his room as he prepared for bed. To accompany his sprightly movements, there came a lively hum from deep within his chest. The tune was a familiar ditty that suited his mood.

When he finally got in bed, the humming sound ceased and he felt a certain peacefulness about him. This was the first time in many, many nights that he had been to bed with any kind of expectation for the coming day. He was quite pleased with himself as he closed his eyes and thought of what was yet to be. Concern for his happiness caused him to anticipate what was to come tomorrow. Happiness was still slumbering someplace beneath a conscious level, but there was wakened hope.

The next day was glorious. The sun was shinning and a light breeze from the Roanoke River drifted across the town common. There were as many people on the common as Sam had ever seen. The entire lot behind Martin's Livery was occupied with wagons, gigs, carriages, and horses were tied up to all the hitching posts. Both sides of King Street were filled with latecomers who could find no other place to leave their teams. By four o'clock, the crowd had grown into a throng. Ladies were dressed in silk and satin with hats of all shapes and sized. Here and there parasols were opened to shade the more delicate ladies. Many had fans which were used to wave to friends as well as to stir the air. Gentlemen in waistcoats knee britches and buckled shoes donned their finest wigs for the occasion. Young boys and girls ran tempestuously among the people. Boys—pulling girl's pigtails, and girls—being flattered that they did—but acting as if they were being brutally attacked, added to the tumult. There were manservants, maidservants, nurses and young lovers here and there in the crowd. Wooden chairs had been brought from the church and the courthouse for the older people. Blankets were being spread on the common for picnics. People in rough smocks and homespun began to meander to the common from Market Street. Many had finished their trading and were becoming a part of all that was happening on the green.

Sam sat next to Jessica and Mrs. Eelbeck on the wooden bench just to the left of the platform that had been erected at the corner of Market and King Street. Directly in front of the platform were four long tables laden with baskets of food.

Jessica looked especially beautiful in her pale blue silk dress that was perhaps a little too revealing at the front. She also had a dark blue fan that she used to point out certain people or to indicate where Sam's attention should be directed. Mrs. Eelbeck had on her finest green silk dress with a large hat that could well protect her from the sun. Sam was in his best clothes. He was aware of the fact that his light brown knee-britches, embroidered waistcoat, white ruffled shirt, black buckled shoes, and dark open coat set off his handsome appearance and that more than one young lady cast interested glances in his direction.

Jessica had temporarily stopped directing his attention and now Sam had the opportunity to notice such people as Allen Jones, his wife and his daughter, Mrs. William R. Davie, standing with John Baptiste Ashe and Elizabeth Montfort Ashe. The family of Willie Jones arrived and joined Allen Jones and his group. Mr. and Mrs. Nicholas Long, the Alstons, and the Martins were among the notable people. It was interesting to Sam that families seemed to gravitate toward other families of the same social standing.

Reverend Ford, who was having difficulty moving through the great congregation of people as he made his way slowly toward the platform, caught Sam's attention. The Reverend was shaking hands, patting the young childrens' heads, and admiring all the lovely gowns of the ladies. When he finally arrived at the platform, he inspected the baskets to make sure there were names on all the family baskets and that the single ladies' baskets were separated from the rest.

Sam was watching the Reverend so closely that he did not see Christopher Dudley come up from behind. Dudley leaned close to Sam as he squatted beside the bench.

"Which one of them baskets is the widow Eelbeck's?" Dudley spoke in a whisper, only loud enough for Sam to hear.

Sam turned and looked questioningly at Dudley. "Why? Do you want to bid on it?"

"Now what other reason would I have for asking, Sam? Everybody knows she's the best cook in Halifax."

"Well, do you see the one with that big yellow bow in front?"

"That's it, huh?" Dudley quickly left while Sam was still looking at the basket with the big yellow bow. With only this bit of information Dudley was off and lost in the crowd. Sam stood and

Strange Wind from the Roanoke

anxiously looked to see where Dudley had gone—but it was to no avail.

Jessica noticed Sam's behavior and Mrs. Eelbeck also became interested.

"What was Christopher Dudley whispering about?" asked Jessica.

"He wanted to know about Mrs. Eelbeck's basket. I was half way through telling him when he shot off like a cannon. I was trying to tell him that it was the basket just to the right of the basket with the big yellow bow—but he didn't let me get beyond asking him if he could see the one with the yellow bow."

"I'd better see if I can find him." Sam got up to leave.

"It's too late, Sam. The auction is beginning," said Jessica, grabbing Sam by the arm and pulling him back to the bench.

Reverend Ford lifted his hands and welcomed all the people. He offer a prayer of thanksgiving for all the food that had been brought to the common. He then began the auction. The large crowd remained reverently quiet.

"We will begin with all the single ladies first. That way we'll get all the young people paired off and the rest of us can eat in peace."

The Reverend quickly auctioned off the first two baskets and now Sam became anxious since the basket with the big yellow bow was the next to be auctioned off.

"How much am I bid for this basket. I am sure whoever made up this basket had someone special in mind," shouted the Reverend, holding the basket high for all to see.

From the edge of the crowd Christopher Dudley let out a loud TWO SHILLINGS—I— OFFER TWO SHILLINGS.

"That's a most gracious offer. Do I hear another bid?" The Preacher listened but no other bid was made.

There was silence. Then, Dudley nudged his rotund body to the front of the table.

From the midst of the crowd, Sam saw a tall girl making her way to the front. She was slim and did not look to weigh more than one hundred pounds. Her smile was something to behold. Two top front teeth were missing. Her red hair only accentuated the large freckles on her face. Sam had never seen her around Halifax. Sam watched her edging her frail frame towards Dudley. Then, Dudley saw her coming just as the Reverend shouted—"SOLD!"

"There's something wrong here," said Dudley, as he looked to the Reverend for some explanation.

Reverend Ford was not aware of what Dudley meant and consentingly handed him the basket. Dudley quickly handed the Reverend two shillings and started toward Sam.

"SAM—SAM—PICKETT—SAM," shouted Dudley as the crowd parted like the Red Sea to make way for him.

Directly behind Dudley came the thin farm girl. "I go wid dat basket. That's mah basket. Wait for me, whoever you may be."

When Dudley reached Sam, the farm girl had caught up with him, and was clutching the handle of the basket that Dudley held.

"Like ah sed, I goes wid the basket," said the farm girl as she smiled warmly at Dudley.

Dudley looked away from Sam to the smiling face. "You take the basket and go with it."

"Ain't cha-going to eat wid me?"

"I was getting the basket for a friend," said Dudley before the girl could get the wrong impression.

"Ah bet you bought it for Slim Jenkins. He's had his eye on mah basket ever since Ah got here," said the girl, as if she understood what Dudley was saying.

"I didn't want it to be known—but—yes —it was Slim who put me up to it," suddenly Dudley realized there was a way out.

"Ah jest knowed it. That Slim Jenkins is all the time messin' wid me. He wah standing rat next to me when mah basket went up for auction and he never lifted a finger to make no bid. Ah might have knowed Slim wah up to somethin'. Ah'm going to find him and spread mah blanket and we're going to have us a picnic rat heah on dis common. Ah won't let on that you told me nothin'—Mr. —ah—Mr—"

"My name is Sam Pickett," said Dudley. "If Slim ever wants to know who bought the basket, just tell him is was Sam Pickett. Now, don't you forget my name is SAM PICKETT."

"Thank you kindly, Mr. Pickett," said the girl. She nodded several times as she stepped back into the crowd.

"What am I going to tell this Slim Jenkins when he comes looking for you?" asked Sam.

"You just tell him it was all your idea. That would be the truth. Sam, I never thought you were capable of doing a thing like this to me," Said Dudley with a threatening look in his usually friendly eyes.

Strange Wind from the Roanoke

"Now wait, Dudley—you just wait—. I was telling you which basket was Mrs. Eelbeck's, but you left before I could finish telling you. I was going to tell you it was the one to the right of the one with the big yellow bow. I just mentioned the basket with the yellow bow to help you locate Mrs. Eelbeck's basket."

"You sure about that, Sam?" Dudley did not seem convinced.

"Dudley, you know me better than that."

The conversation was abruptly interrupted as Mrs. Eelbeck held up two baskets of food.

"Sam gave me the money to purchase my basket when he bought Jessica's basket. So, that makes you two about even, I would say."

When they were all settled on the blanket to enjoy the food, Sam wondered if he would now have to become a religious man in order to get the full value for all the money he had spent. After purchasing two baskets and spending four shillings, he felt that he had greatly contributed to the new addition at Reverend Ford's church.

Sam had enough food left to make a basket for Benjamin McCullen—so he excused himself long enough to take the food to the jail.

As he walked back to the common from his brief visit with McCullen, he was thoroughly aware of the excited feeling that now possessed him and caused him to hurry back to be in the company of Jessica Jackson.

Chapter 4

It was early October when Sam's employer, William R. Davie, returned to Halifax. From the time of his return until the latter part of December, Davie was beset with impending obligations to the state and to his law practice. Soon after returning to Halifax, he became the lawyer for the Plaintiff in the case of Bayard and wife v. Singleton, which was being tried at New Bern. This case involved a suit to recover property that had been confiscated from Bayard's wife during the Revolutionary War. During this time, he was elected to the House of Commons as the Federalist delegate from Halifax. Because of previous obligations, Davie did not arrive at its meeting in Tarboro until December the fifth. Although many other issues were brought before the Assembly, perhaps the most important action was the calling of a state convention to be held at Hillsborough.

Correspondence to friends throughout the state now demanded much of Davie's time. Sam was constantly writing letters to different leaders with information that Davie felt needed to be communicated. Davie penned many personal letters to close friends, such as James Iredell, Samuel Johnston, Hugh Williamston and William Dobbs Spaight. Almost all the letters urged the new delegates to read closely the new Constitution and to be prepared to defend its merits at the upcoming convention. In many cases, Davie stated his personal views

Strange Wind from the Roanoke

as to the great need of its ratification. It became imperative that all delegates have a copy to study before the plan was put before the Hillsborough Convention.

It had been a cold winter, but now in late March of 1788, the sun was beginning to warm the earth and except for the gusty winds, the weather was tolerable.

Sam sat at a small desk next to Davie's large desk copying a letter that was to be mailed to Samuel Johnston. He had been writing so many letters these past few months, that he hardly had time to discuss any law cases with Davie. He felt fortunate, though, to be in the same office with such a distinguished man. Even though Davie was only thirty-three years old, he had accomplished more than many men who had lived long beyond those years. His reputation in the service of his country during the great revolution was common knowledge to all who knew Davie.

Sam enjoyed the stories that Davie told about the Constitutional Convention. He was constantly being made aware of the great influence Benjamin Franklin had with all the other members. He spoke highly of Alexander Hamilton and James Madison. He even mention the fact that the absence of Thomas Jefferson was sorely felt. Perhaps his favorite story was the one about the carving on the back of George Washington's chair. The top slat of the back of the chair had a carving of a "sun". Franklin made the statement that artist and carvers of wood always had a problem in distinguishing between a "rising "and a "setting" sun. He told Madison that he had often wondered if the sun on the back of Washington's chair was a "rising" or a "setting" sun. Now with the completion of the Constitution he was confident to know that it was a "rising" sun. This was only one of the stories that Davie told but it was one of Sam's favorites. Davie did not fail to mention that the Convention was in danger of failure many times and Washington and Franklin were the two who made sure of its success.

Soon after the war Davie had moved to Halifax to start his law practice. When he and Sarah Jones were married, they had lived for two years at Mount Gallant in Northampton County at the home of his father-in-law, Allen Jones. Then in 1783, the two moved to Halifax and built a home on St. David Street and called it "Loretta".

Sam looked up from his letter at Davie, who was busy at a letter of his own. Davie had a superior authority about him and his dark eyes scanning the paper before him were keenly intelligent. His dark hair was swept across his ears and his perfectly shaped nose enhanced his oval face. He was a tall man in more ways than just physical stature. His voice was deep and mellow, but he spoke quietly when he was not giving a speech. He was a gentleman who had mastered all the social graces. Sam had heard from others that Davie could be most demanding when he spoke for a cause. From Sam's relationship with Davie, he knew that Davie was a thorough man when he prepared a case or if he was planning any kind of presentation.

"What time is it, Sam?" Davie looked up from his letter as he leaned back in his chair to stretch.

"I know what you're thinking. It's time for these letters to be posted."

"The five o'clock stage should be here soon."

"I never knew there were so many men involved in politics before I started addressing all these letters," said Sam.

"We've only scratched the surface, Sam. I promised John Ashe I'd meet him at Martin's Tavern and get four copies of the new Constitution to him. I'll drop the letters off at Dudley's —that is if you're finished."

"This is the last one." Sam held up the letter that he had just addressed.

"Good. Then I'll be on my way. I'll be back just as soon as I give these copies of the Constitution to Ashe."

The new Constitution was what Davie was so concerned about these days and consequently, was demanding most of his time. Davie reached to the rack just to his left and quickly struggled into his coat, picked up the letters as he passed Sam's desk, and hurried out of the office.

Sam had been at his desk all afternoon and now thought it would be a good time to stretch his legs. He stood at his desk and then walked to the front window. A brisk wind was blowing and the branches of the white oaks across the street were bending and dancing as they swayed in rhythm. There was a tempo to the rise and fall of the gusts that was much like music. Two men hurried from behind Martin's Livery toward Market Street. Looking toward the cemetery, Sam could see a man standing at Josie's grave. At first, Sam thought he was kneeling —then he thought he was praying. Then he realized

Strange Wind from the Roanoke

that the man was reading words on the slab. He was well dressed and no doubt a gentleman. Watching from the window, Sam took the sleeve of his shirt and wiped the moisture from the pane so he could get a better view. This was no ordinary gentleman. There was something about the man—he looked—familiar—then Sam said out loud—"Why, I believe that's John Hamilton. It is John Hamilton." Sam startled himself. Even as he spoke the words, the gentleman began walking from the cemetery toward Davie's office. There was a confidence in his upright stride that bespoke the manner of a gentleman. His walk was not like the common man who moved at a pace suited to one to his station and destination.

Sam looked about the office as if he wanted to find some place to hide. Then, gathering his composure, he walked slowly to his desk and sat down.

Soon the man was at the door.

"Come in." Sam stood at his desk as the door opened.

"Is this the office of the Lawyer William R. Davie?" Hamilton took the cocked hat from his head.

"Yes, Sir." Sam looked closely at Hamilton and there was no hint that Hamilton recognized him. There were faded scars on Hamilton's face. Smallpox evidently had left those marks.

"Well, then I assume you are Mr. Davie"

"No, Mr. Hamilton. I'm Sam Pickett."

"Sam—Sam—Sam Pickett." With arms outstretched, he came closer to Sam. Sam stepped from behind the desk and welcomed Hamilton with a gentle hug. There was an enigmatic smile on Sam's face as he embraced his father-in-law.

Hamilton stood back from Sam and looked at him. "I should have recognized you, Sam. But—but—it's been quite a while since I've seen you. I shall never forget that night you came to my house to warn us that we were about to be arrested. We would have been, too, if we had stayed until morning."

"Sit down, Sir. Let me have your coat and hat." Sam extended his hand as he spoke.

"I've just come from the cemetery," said Hamilton, handing Sam his hat and coat.

"I know, I saw you from the window."

"It's been what —-ten —eleven years, since we left Halifax." Hamilton tried to remember.

"Closer to twelve, Sir." Sam put Hamilton's hat and coat on the rack.

"Dudley told me where Josie was put to rest."

"I heard you were in Petersburg, but I never could get an address. When Josie died, I tried every way I could to locate you." Sam thought of the letter that Reverend Ford had delivered and how he had never acknowledged it. He quickly satisfied a guilty feeling by realizing that even now he did not know what to say to Mr. John Hamilton.

"I've known about her death for some time now. Word reached me in Petersburg about the epidemic in Edenton. You know, the news about smallpox travels about as fast as the disease."

"I see you contracted the disease yourself." Sam noticed the scars on Hamilton's face.

"I had it during the war while I was in the service of the King. My case was mild one. I was lucky."

"I had no idea death could come so quickly." Sam remembered.

"Josie wrote to me while she was in Edenton. Just after she came down with the disease." Hamilton seemed hesitant to say anymore.

For some reason that was beyond his comprehension, Sam felt that John Hamilton wanted to tell him more.

"I have her last letter to me. Would you like to read it?" Offered Sam.

"I would be most grateful."

Without standing, Sam reached to his coat on the rack and handed Hamilton the faded letter. He watched with keen interest as Hamilton slowly read each word of the worn letter. Tears began to swell in his father-in-law's eyes. Upon completing the reading, he gently folded the letter and placed it back inside the envelope, wiped the sleeve of his shirt across his cheeks, and handed the letter to Sam.

"I had good intentions to come back to Halifax before now, but I've been in the service of the King and have been unable to leave Boston until now. I was, perhaps more aware of the fact that I would not have been welcomed here, Sam."

"I can't speak for all the people, but I'm happy to see you, Sir. So, you're still in the service of the King."

Strange Wind from the Roanoke

"Oh, yes. I'm His Majesty's Consul for the state of Massachusetts."

"What brings you back to Halifax?"

"I'm here on personal business with Mr. Davie. I understand there just might be some chance of getting my property back. I have been corresponding with my brother Archibald. He managed to hold on to his property. But, then he never joined up with the British. I suppose his loyalties paid off in the long run. I hope to see him when I get to New Bern."

Hamilton turned as Sam looked toward the front door. Davie entered.

"I met Ashe just as I left Dudley's, so I thought I'd come on back to the office."

There was an irascible look on Davie's face and Sam wondered if any introduction was in order.

"Mr. Davie, this is Mr. John Hamilton. Mr. Hamilton—Mr. Davie." Sam noticed Davie's expression changed to a smile that seemed to be pretentious.

"Sit down, Mr. Hamilton. We're happy to have you here in Halifax. I've heard a great deal about you," Davie said courteously.

"Well, the war is over. Maybe we can forget about all you've heard."

"I understand you served your country well. You were in Georgia, I believe," said Davie.

"The same time as you. I understand you were wounded at Stono Ferry." Hamilton looked closely to Davie's reaction.

"On my twenty-third birthday. Well, now, how can I be of service to you, Sir?" Davie showed no hint of bitterness for the former Loyalist and enemy.

"Your name was brought to my attention by several men whose opinion I respect. You've adapted to civilian life better than most." Hamilton seemed impressed.

"I suppose we all have to forgive if we are ever to forget," said Davie.

"I understand that there may be some hope of getting my property back," said Hamilton, getting to the business at hand.

Sam stood. "Would it suit you better if I left, Mr. Hamilton?"

"No—no, Sam. I have nothing to keep from you"

"I would like for Sam to hear what I'm about to tell you, Mr. Hamilton. So I appreciate your confidence in Sam."

"Oh, Sam and I have never kept any secrets from each other."

"Thank you, Sir." Sam sat back down and listened.

Davie looked searchingly at Hamilton and continued.

"There was a case that was decided just this past November that bears great resemblance to your own situation. Do you know of the Bayard and Wife versus Singleton Case:"

"No, I've not heard of the case," said Hamilton, shaking his head.

"Well, it seems that a Mr. Samuel Cornell of New Bern left this state in 1775 and returned in 1777 as a British citizen. When he heard that New Bern was in a state of change, he decided to transfer all his property to his daughter. This he did on the ship which took him to England. Some months ago, the daughter, a Mrs. Bayard, entered a suit in court to regain her property.

"What did the court decide?" Hamilton could well see that the case was similar to that of his own.

"Let me finish. Iredell, Johnston and I argued for Bayard and wife on the basis that the Confiscation Act of the State Legislature violated the right of trial by jury which is guaranteed in our state Constitution."

"If one is right and lawful, then the other has to be contradictory," agreed Hamilton.

"Well, it so happened that the court could not reach a decision. The case was then referred back to the legislature for review. When the legislative committee reported, it referred the case back to the court. The court decision has just recently been handed down and it does set a precedent. The court over-ruled the Legislative Act of 1785, which stated that such cases could not be heard in courts. To my knowledge, this is the first time the court has set aside an act of the legislature. Sam, you should remember this is a first."

"No court has ever done that before?" Sam seemed amazed.

"Not to my knowledge. That's not all the court decided, however. In November of this past year, it was determined that aliens cannot hold land, and if they do, it must be forfeited to the sovereign. This means, of course, that all Loyalists can sue for recovery of their lands and property and it will be handled by the court. But the court has ruled against the recovery by aliens."

Strange Wind from the Roanoke

"There seems to be little hope for my property, then," said Hamilton.

"There's still a chance the courts will someday rule otherwise, but I must be truthful with you, Sir. Many cases have been pending in the courts, such as your own, have been taken off the docket."

"I suppose the only recourse I have is to hope for some change of attitude of the courts. Is it possible to leave my case in your hands. If there should ever come the opportunity, I would appreciate your service."

Hamilton stood and reached across the desk to shake hands with Davie, who gave a consenting nod, as he took his hand.

"Mr. Hamilton, would you care to come to Mrs. Eelbeck's to stay the night?" Sam asked the question as he extended his hand.

"I understand that's the best place to stay—if it still has the same reputation it had twelve years ago. I could do with a good meal."

"Sam, I suggest we close for the day. Come, I'll walk with you as far as St. David's." Davie reached for his coat as he spoke.

Davie handed Mr. Hamilton's his hat and coat and soon the three were walking down King Street towards the Boarding House.

Just as they approached the corner of Market and King, a large group of men were milling about on the common.

"Wonder what's going on?" Sam looked to Davie, who only shook his head.

Stopping momentarily, all three could see a pole about ten feet high and from it dangled a dummy with the name of JOHN HAMILTON written in red sprawling letters on a poster which hung from its neck.

"Sam, I think you'd better let me do the talking," suggested Davie, as he stepped just ahead of Sam and John Hamilton.

Jesse Turner, Harry Bedlow, Christopher Dudley and about twenty other men stood in front of the dummy of John Hamilton.

"Word travels fast when it reaches Dudley's Tavern. You did say you went by there before you came to the office, didn't you?" Sam could see a bewildered look on Hamilton's face.

"There was hardly anyone at the tavern when I stopped by. I just asked Dudley where Josie was buried."

Sam and Hamilton stopped talking as Davie walked up to the men.

"What are you fellows up to?" Davie looked at the different faces as he spoke.

Jesse Turner came forward as spokesman for the group. "I thought better of you Davie. You ain't particular about the company you keep." Sam remembered the expression when Turner was having fun with Looney Oney.

"You ain't welcomed in this here town, Hamilton!" came a shout from one of the men.

"You've been run outa town one time. How many times we got to do it before you take heed?" Harry Bedlow held his clinched fist high above his head as he shouted.

"I have a right to be where I want to be. I am here in the service of the King. I have credentials to show. You can't run me out of town." John Hamilton was not to be intimidated.

"Don't tell me Harry Bedlow can't run you outa town. If he can run his old lady outa town, he can run anybody out," shouted one of Jesse's cronies.

Davie turned and pointed in Hamilton's direction. "This man has a right to travel anywhere—just as all of you have the same right. The war has run its course. Now it's time for you all to realize that Hamilton is no longer our enemy."

"You've got a short memory, Davie. That's all I got to say," shouted Jesse.

Davie held his ground. "This man lost a young son in the war and has come to Halifax to visit the resting place of his beloved daughter, Josie. Have any of you lost so much? I know he was on the wrong side and many of our soldiers died because of him. But that is in the past. John Hamilton has come to Halifax not wishing to harm any of you. He is an official of the King of England and while he is here, he will be treated with the courtesy and respect that we would extend to any other official from any other country."

"You mean he didn't come back here to make trouble about his property?" asked Dudley, stepping forward to make his presence known.

"All of you should know what the law is regarding Tory property. How many Tories have regained their property?" Davie waited for a response from the men.

Dudley looked to the men. There was silence. "Just so long as I don't have to set eyes on you no more. You stay away from my tavern, you hear."

"And don't be out on the streets tonight or you'll be hanging from that pole just like the other dummy," shouted one of the men.

"You men don't have to be concerned about where Mr. Hamilton will spend the night. Come along, Sam—Mr. Hamilton." Davie motioned for them to follow.

There was still a noisy rumbling of discontent among the men as the three continued down King Street.

"What do you think they'll do?" Sam asked, as they walked along the street.

"Mr. Hamilton will be my guest tonight, Sam. No harm will come to him at my house."

"Oh, I almost forgot about my horse and gig at Martin's Livery," said Hamilton, looking back.

"Just keep walking. Sam can bring your horse to my house later when the men leave the common." Said Davie in a matter of fact manner.

When they reached St. David's Street, Hamilton and Davie turned right and Sam continued to Mrs. Eelbeck's Boarding House.

Being anxious to get John Hamilton's horse and gig to Davie's house, Sam hurried through his supper. Soon after he had finished, he asked Jessica if she would walk with him to the common. If anyone should ask him about Hamilton, he would just pretend that he and Jessica were out for a stroll, and he would say that Hamilton was spending the night at Davie's home. On the way to the livery stable, Sam explained all that had happened that afternoon. As they came to the common, there were only the charred remains of the dummy of John Hamilton. It had been burned in effigy. Sam was happy to see that the town common was almost deserted.

"I thought that we might just run into Mr. Hedgepeth—but—I suppose it's a little late for him to be out." Sam looked at Jessica.

"He'll be staying later when the days get longer," said Jessica, knowing the old man's habit when the season changed.

Sam and Jessica walked across King Street to the livery and were told that John Hamilton had paid the keeper for that one day and that day was spent at sundown. After much explaining, Sam was finally able to convince the keeper that he had been sent by William

R. Davie to fetch the horse and gig. It was always interesting to Sam how quickly common men reacted to the name of William R. Davie.

When the horse was hitched to the gig, Sam and Jessica climbed aboard. Since the seat had been designed for only one person, Jessica had to sit very close to Sam. The warmth of her body touched feelings deep within Sam. Sam let the horse walk down the railed-fence road to King Street. Sam was comfortable with the thought that he did not need to hurry.

Two men were sitting at the corner of the common. They watched Sam and Jessica, and Sam could tell by their reactions that he two were interested in what they saw. Sam nodded to the men as if he expected them to return the salutation. There was no acknowledgment, but words passed between the two men.

Soon they were turning off King Street onto St. David's. It was a short drive to William R. Davie's home. On each side of the street were several white wooden houses with brick chimneys. Located about half way down St. David Street was one of the most interesting buildings in Halifax, the Royal White Hart Lodge. Each time he passed this special building, Sam felt a reverence for the great man resting inside the only grave in the front yard. Here the remains of Joseph Montfort were lying protected by an iron fence that extended along the perimeter of the plot. Inside the wrought iron fence was a slab of marble which told of his greatness: CLERK OF THE COURT—COLONEL OF THE MILITIA—MASONIC LEADER OF THE ROYAL WHITE HART LODGE—THE FIRST GRAND MASTER OF AMERICA. Sam thought of all those legal papers and wills of people that Davie served. Since he was clerk of the court, Joseph Montfort's name appeared on almost all the legal documents.

Sam continued to look to his left at the Masonic Lodge,

"Now there was a man who knew how to live."

"No one would argue with you about that. I don't know of anyone who didn't look up to him," added Jessica.

"He's one to be remembered. Too bad he never lived to see us win our freedom from England."

Sam wondered if Jessica understood that he was trying to find some meaning and purpose to his own life. To Sam, Joseph Montfort was the kind of man he would want to imitate.

Turning left off St. David Street, Sam drove by the house to the back, where the stables were located. Behind the large two-story

Strange Wind from the Roanoke

house was a smokehouse, a carriage house, and a special stable for Allen Jones' great horse, Midnight. Then, there were the servant's quarters, and just beyond this building were as many a fourteen huts where Davie's slaves were quartered. Two mulatto women watched from the small porch of the servant's quarters and several black children bundled up in homespun played along the road that continued toward the open fields. Smoke was coming from the chimneys as the slave women prepared food for their families.

After the horse was tied up at the stables, Sam and Jessica stopped long enough to admire the magnificent "Midnight."

"This horse is the most valuable horse in all of this province," said Sam as he stroked the nose of the large black stallion.

"What makes him so valuable?" Jessica seemed interested.

"It's his blood line. I've heard that Mr. Jones gets as much as twenty shillings each time his horse is "at stud".

Jessica thought it absurd that any horse should be that valuable.

As they walked to the front of the house, Sam tried to explain that the value of the horse was something that had been determined by those who "knew" horses. Allen Jones had acquired Midnight after he had seen him race in Warren County. He stabled his horse at Willie Jones' stables and it was at that time that Sam worked with the horse at the track. Soon after Mr. Jones had brought Midnight to Halifax, there was a challenge from a Duckenfield man in Edenton who wanted to match his chestnut called "Golden Boy" against Midnight in a one-mile heat. The "one mile heat" was a race that Midnight had been trained to run.

When Sam thought about that time in his past, he could hardly believe that fourteen years had passed since that day. After that race against the Duckenfield's horse from Edenton, Allen Jones put Midnight out for "stud". That was the reason the stallion was at Davie's stables.

Sam continued to explain that the value of the horse was relative—and the value would change as conditions changed.

Jessica seemed pleased that Sam understood the way she thought. There was even a hint in Sam's explanation that he agreed with her.

When they came to the front of the house, Hamilton and Davie were sitting on the porch. Sam told them that the dummy had been burned at the town common, and it was quickly decided that John Hamilton should leave Halifax at the first light of day.

As Jessica and Sam walked back to Mrs. Eelbeck's, Sam talked of what he considered the most important values in his life. Coming to the White Hart Lodge, Sam spoke of Joseph Montfort and his daughters. Mary had married Willie Jones and Elizabeth had married John Baptiste Ashe, and both marriages seemed to be thriving. Sam used these two marriages to explain what he considered necessary in making a good union.

It was getting dark when they turned off St. David's onto King Street, but they saw no need to hurry.

Sam felt a need to know what Jessica thought. "What do you consider necessary for a good and lasting marriage, Jessica?"

"There must be love and understanding, to say the least," said Jessica, looking to see Sam's reaction.

"And how about money and property?"

"There should be enough to satisfy the needs. I think it greatly depends on what is desired in life."

"There have been many marriages right here in Halifax that have been made on the basis of money and property alone—without love ever being considered. You know, my marriage to Josie Hamilton might never have been possible if it hadn't been for the Revolution.

"The war certainly changed the way people feel about Tories." Jessica remembered.

"I was never accepted by the Hamiltons before the war. Then, the war came and the Hamiltons were not accepted by anybody in Halifax."

"I suppose some people will never be accepted —even if the law changes there are those who will always think that they are better than anybody else."

Sam thought of John Hamilton, Looney Oney and the many slaves who were held in bondage.

Then, Sam became aware that they were approaching the boarding house and he had not mentioned the one thing he had been on his mind.

"Jessica, there's something that's been bothering me for quite some time and I'd like to ask you what you think."

"What's bothering you, Sam?"

Strange Wind from the Roanoke

"I know it may not make any sense to you but I've been having this strange dream about Josie's funeral. There's not a week that goes by that I don't have it. It's always the same."

"I can understand that, Sam. I remember waking at night from the nightmare about the time the British came to Halifax and completely destroyed our Ordinary. Even now, it returns to haunt me. It takes time, Sam."

"Maybe we both need to think more about the present. If we don't help ourselves, we can't expect others to care about us."

"What do you suggest, Sam?"

"Well, I used to love to fish. Why don't we pack us a lunch and go down to Quanky Creek? I know the exact spot. Will you come with me?"

Jessica's eyes showed excitement. "I'll see if I can find someone to tend my shop. But you must promise me one thing before I agree."

"What's that?" Sam felt defeated in his effort.

"That you won't get mad if I catch the biggest fish."

"I promise—I promise —just as soon as things get back to normal, we'll see who can catch the biggest fish," came Sam's quick reply.

When they arrived at Mrs. Eelbeck's, Sam said goodbye to Jessica at the door. He held her hand and gave it a slight squeeze and was pleased to feel a strong response accentuated with a special smile as Jessica moved away.

Sam decided to sit a while on the front porch before he retired. Weather permitting, this had become one of his daily rituals. He was pleased with the understanding he had gained from his talk with Jessica. Sitting in the rocker, he became very relaxed and pensive. He thought of the attitude of the men at the common, then of the great interest Davie had in the Federal Constitution. He recalled Davie had mention that the question of slavery had to be postponed at the Constitutional Convention. With the passing of the "three-fifths compromise" it was agreed that the slaves would be counted as three-fifths of a person for the purpose of taxation and for the purpose of representation in the House of Representatives. It was agreed that each slave owner would deal with the "slavery question" as he saw fit. Several leaders at the Constitutional Convention were dubious about even considering the question of slavery. Many were of the opinion that a Constitution would never be finished if the question of slavery was not postponed. Some had agreed that they would never sell any of their slaves. Many slave owners stated that their slaves were better off than those who were sold "down river". These were sent back to the sugar field of the West Indies.

    Davie had told Sam that Thomas Jefferson had willed that his slaves be free when he died. Jefferson had also provided that those who were not prepared to leave the plantation would be allowed to stay as long as was needed. Sam did not own a slave and he was always sympathetic and conscious of the treatment they got from their overseers and masters. Sam had always assumed that the treatment greatly depended on the character of the slave owner and the overseer. There were some slaves who were manumitted because of some act of bravery or some great deed that brought honor to their name. Whatever the relationship, Sam concluded that it was an institution that would one day be abolished. There were many ways the slaveowners justified their right of ownership. Whatever those reasons were, they were not good enough. Sam thought that the slaves would have to prepare for what would one day be their independence. Now, the leaders were proposing a plan of government that would have to be accepted by the people. In so many ways his life was analogous, for he, too, was now searching for some basic plan upon which he could begin to build his life —again.

CHAPTER 5

When he finally got to bed, he thought of the way his life was taking shape. He recalled the time in his life that made his relationship with Allen Jones so special. His life had not been the same since that glorious day. Allen Jones became his benefactor and was like a father to him after that day.

Sam's thoughts of that special time were slowly becoming a dream.

It was the day he had sat on Allen Jones' horse, Midnight, in the mile heat (race) against Nathaniel Duckenfield's "Golden Boy". Duckenfield's supporters from Edenton and Allen Jones' supporters from Northampton and Halifax County had bet heavily on their favorite horses. Sam had worked with Midnight at Willie Jones' racetrack and knew the horse's temperament. There seemed to be an understanding between him and Midnight. Sam could tell when Midnight wanted to move and he also knew when to hold his horse in check. "Good communications" is what Allen Jones called it.

That was some day—that day. It had been about twelve years since the race and Sam could remember each detail as it happened. He had relived the event many times and each time he remembered more than he had the time before. The park at "The Grove" was teeming with spectators who brought picnic lunches. Some special friends of the Jones had been staying at "Grove House" for several days prior to the "Big" race. At the back of "Grove House" was a large bay window from which many of Willie Jones' special guests could view the race.

Notices were posted in all the surrounding towns announcing the event. A mile "Heat" was an unusually long distance. Four times around the quarter-mile track was demanding too much of any horse, so Sam had heard from the quarter-horse owners. The quarter-mile races were held during the morning and many good horses were shown. The main event was the "mile heat" scheduled for the afternoon. That race was the reason for the crowd. Small bets were placed on favorite horses and fellowship prevailed among the men from both towns during the morning. However, just before the main event, the Halifax crowd assembled on the side of the racetrack next to "Grove House". On the opposite side of the track, the Edenton crowd anxiously waited for their horse to appear. There seemed to be something magnetic about the way the crowd polarized for the coming event. Fellowship was quickly forgotten as shouts and jeers were heard coming from both sides of the track.

Sam was with Uncle Louie at Midnight's stall but Midnight's rider was nowhere in sight.

"Where's Johnny Turnbill?" Sam asked. "The race will be starting before he's given "Midnight" his "warm-up"

"Don't know but Mr. Jones will reckon wid him." Answered Uncle Louie.

Sam looked again and could see Allen Jones walking briskly toward them. Midnight's owner was dressed in different shades of green that day. His pants were light green and complimented his darker green coat. His cocked hat was a shade darker than his coat. No one could mistake the striking figure of Mr. Allen Jones. Many avid supporters, including his brother, Willie, followed him. People stepped aside and made way for them. Sam saw a troubled look in Allen Jones' eyes and knew immediately that something was wrong.

"We need a rider," began Allen Jones, "Johnny Turnbill was at Dudley's last night and early this morning prematurely celebrating his victory."

"Call the race off, Allen," suggested one of his supporters, who had perhaps bet too heavily on the race.

Strange Wind from the Roanoke

"We cannot let our supporters down," came the quick reply from Allen Jones.

"Is he able to ride at all," asked Sam.

"He's in a drunken stupor. He'll never race again. I'll see to that. I've warned him about his drinking. I shouldn't have placed so much trust in the rascal."

"What can we do now, Sir?" asked Sam.

There was no answer.

Sam looked at the downcast faces of the men around him. They were dejected and had no suggestions. Sam looked to Uncle Louie, but the old man looked away. Turning again to Allen Jones, Sam saw a gleam of hope that suddenly lightened Jones' eyes.

"There is but one hope. Sam, you must ride Midnight. It's our only chance to win this race. There has always been an understanding between you and that horse. Maybe your feeling for Midnight will be enough to compensate for the skill of the Duckenfield rider. You're heavier than Turnbill but Midnight can carry you. You've ridden him enough and he's a strong horse." Allen Jones made the statement as if it were all settled.

"That boy's thirty pounds heavier than the other rider. He'll never make the last lap," said one of the men.

"I say I know my horse and I say we race," said Allen Jones.

"Well, I'm not betting my money on that kind of odds," said the man as he walked away.

Allen Jones turned to his supporters. "You all do what you think is best with your money. I'll take all the bets you men want to change. If you have doubts about the race."

Willie Jones had not voiced his opinion but now he stepped forward. "What bets my brother does not see fit to cover I'll gladly take." He turned to the men who were no longer supporters. "You men spread the word through the crowd and if anyone wants to change his bet send him to me."

The men scurried through the crowd to tell the people of the change that had to be made in race.

Sam knew without any doubt that the race was on. That moment—oh—that moment—the world suddenly began to whirl. As if by an Act of God, he was thrust from a mere stable boy to that glorious position on Midnight's back. A lump came to his throat. He swallowed—the lump remained.

"Mr. Jones, I love that horse," the words seemed inadequate, but Sam could muster nothing more at that moment.

"Well, let us hope that love conquers all," philosophized Allen Jones, as he turned to Uncle Louie. "Get Midnight saddled and ready for the race."

"I'll do my best and I pray that it will be good enough." Said Sam, not really knowing what to say.

"Uncle Louie, get the boots and that blue jacket for Sam," ordered Allen Jones.

Sam sat on a stool, pulled the boots on quickly and stood for Uncle Louie, who was holding the blue jacket.

Uncle Louie cupped his hands and Sam was catapulted onto Midnight's back.

Allen Jones inspected the bridle and the saddle. "Let him have his way when you come to the last lap. Don't hold him back. Just let him have his way. He knows the way home."

The world had not stopped whirling, whirling. Sam let Midnight trot to the track. There was a great roar from the Halifax side of the track, and Sam slowed Midnight to a walk? Midnight pranced haughtily as they waited for the Duckenfield rider. The strong body between his legs gave Sam confidence that his horse was ready. He pulled reins and held his horse. He wanted Midnight to feel peaked by the time the flag was dropped. Sam felt there was as anxiousness beneath him that he had not experienced before with Midnight. Perhaps the race had excited his horse too much. He spoke softly, and it seemed to calm Midnight.

Golden Boy was brought to the track and a swell of cheers came from the Edenton crowd. The great chestnut had a professional rider. The cheers were deafening, as the red-jacket rider trotted Golden Boy before the Edenton supporters.

Two riders on lead horses came on the track and led the two racehorses to the starting post. Sam could feel a nervousness in himself as well as the unsteadiness of Midnight. Before Sam could get Midnight settled for the start, the flag was down and Golden Boy was off. Sam tightened his legs and was off. It was a poor start for Midnight. The chestnut was ahead. To his right, Sam could see blurred faces, flying hats and waving arms. They were galloping through the backstretch. Sam could feel the flowing power beneath him as he stared at the hindquarters of Golden Boy. A hail of gravel pelted Sam's face. He was temporarily blinded. He had not expected this. They were to the far end of the track and Sam's blurred vision cleared enough for him to see the faces of the spectators who were leaning on the rail. He sat steady with a firm grip on the reins.

"Three more laps," came a yell from the gate near the starting post.

Sam forgot his nervousness and leaned forward. "Not yet, not just yet. I'll tell you when—" He was moving— riding,— hurling through space. Midnight pulled at the bit. Sam restrained him. He knew his horse.

"Go easy, boy. Go easy. We've got a long way to go. Half of the race is ahead of us."

"Two laps to go," came the yell from the side, as they rounded the track for the last half of the race.

The chestnut began to put more space between them at the beginning of the third lap. Sam thought that Golden Boy was at top speed. He hoped that Golden Boy was at top speed. The gap between the two horses lengthened and Sam was a good four lengths behind.

"One lap to go." He had passed the starting post for the third time. They were beginning the final lap.

Sam let the reins loose and yelled to his horse. "Now. MIDNIGHT, NOW—NOW." He felt a surge beneath him and the space between the two horses began to diminish. He leaned forward and let Midnight have his way. Sam remembered Allen Jones' advice.

"Homestretch," someone yelled, as the horses rounded the turn.

The chestnut ahead was gathering speed as the red-jacket rider began whipping his horse. Midnight was gathering more speed. Sam was riding—riding—then—closing—closing. The two horses were now side by side. Midnight continued to gather speed. Sam had never ridden so fast. The two horses were straining for the lead. The two riders were straining—straining. The professional and the amateur were side by side and straining. Sam suddenly felt his horse ease forward. There was a quick look of surprise on the face of the professional as Midnight moved ahead. The great Golden Boy was a good length behind as the horses finished the "one-mile heat."

When he rode Midnight to the Halifax side, George and Josie came from the crowd and seemed even happier than he as they ushered him to his Halifax supporters. The spinning world seemed to gain momentum as he was boosted on the shoulders of two men and held high above the cheering crowd. To Sam that was the most important day of his life. Both Allen and Willie profited from the race. Allen Jones never let Sam forget how grateful he was for the victory. That was the day that Sam entered into a special relationship that would be with him for the rest of his life.

Sam was still thinking about his dream the next morning as he walked with quickened steps along King Street. There was much to be done at the office now that the leaders throughout the province were considering the Constitution. Davie wanted the word sent to all his friends so they would be aware of his support of the great document.

As Sam came to the corner of King and Market Street, he became concerned about the group of men and women who were congregated on the town common. It was unusual to see so many so early in the morning. As he drew near, he heard a man yell to another who was also approaching the crowd. "Harry Bedlow caught him trying to sneak outa town before the sun rose this morning."

Sam's heart was beating fast as he pushed his way through the crowd. Coming to the opening, he saw John Hamilton had been put in the stock. Hamilton's head and arms poked through the opening as he stood helplessly facing the jeering crowd. His clothes were smeared with tar and feathers stuck to his pants and shirt in patches. He was a pitiable sight to behold. There was no semblance of the gentleman that Sam had first seen coming from the cemetery. As sad as the spectacle was to Sam, he could not help but think that Hamilton looked like a half-picked chicken.

Sam's keen eyes quickly scanned the crowd to locate the sheriff but Bob Whitehead was nowhere to be seen. Just as Sam looked back down King Street, he saw the sheriff coming toward the common.

"Sheriff, they've put John Hamilton in the pillory at the common!"

"So that's the reason for the crowd." Bob Whitehead did not seem as disturbed as Sam had thought he would be.

"You've got to make them set him free."

"I have no way to control that bunch, Sam. It would take a militia to make them go home."

"Well, somebody had better do something. Those men aren't about to let him go. They're so riled up they're liable to do anything."

Strange Wind from the Roanoke

"Until he's harmed in some way, I'm not about to interfere. There's too many of them, Sam. They're just having a little fun with him. I don't know for sure that he don't deserve all that he's gittin'."

"What you're saying is you'd rather wait and see if any harm comes to Hamilton."

"I'm saying I'm not about to stop them. I don't know if I would if I could."

Sam turned and hurried back to the common. He thought there must be some way to disperse the crowd. As he was walking back an idea flashed in his mind. At the edge of the town, Dudley's tavern-boy was talking excitedly with one of his friends about all that was happening. Sam slowly came up behind the two boys.

After quickly laying out his plan to the two, Sam slipped each of the boys a shiny coin. The two boy's eyes lit up as they grabbed the coin and immediately ran among the people shouting—-SLAVE REBELLION—-WILLIE JONES' SLAVES HEADED FOR HALIFAX—OVER A HUNDRED OF'EM. GIT TO YOUR HOMES—— GIT TO YOUR CHILDREN—SLAVE REBELLION. These words struck fear in the minds of people faster than any other words that Sam had ever heard.

Sam stood back from the crowd and watched his scheme being put into action. He was astounded how quickly the common was cleared. Men and women began yelling and calling to their loved ones as they hurried from the common to their homes. The two boys strolled down Market Street as if they were the only brave ones left in town. Sam hurried to John Hamilton. He took his knife and slashed the rope that secured one end of the stock that shackled Hamilton. He lifted the wooden beam and Hamilton freed his arms and head.

"Hurry back to Mrs. Eelbeck's stable. Take the black mare. She's my horse. Hurry now!"

"I won't forget this, Sam. I'm in your debt."

"You need to stay away from Halifax. People here have good memories."

"I don't intend to come this way again. Thank you, Sam."

With these words, John Hamilton ran along King Street towards Mrs. Eelbeck's. He seemed to be looking in all directions as he hurried away from the common.

Sam slowly walked along the now deserted street to Davie's office.

About an hour later, Davie came to the office. Sam was busy writing a letter for Davie to sign.

"Hear about the slave rebellion, Sam?" Davie walked to his desk.

"What slave rebellion!"

"Oh, seems that some children started a rumor about Willie Jones' slaves. Scared the people so badly, they're still inside their houses—not a soul on the streets. People ought to know that slaves on Willie Jones' plantation are treated better than the slaves on any other plantation in this province."

"Rumors are sometimes more powerful than the truth and sometimes makes the listener afraid." Sam looked back at the letter he was writing.

"You're right about that, Sam. When we are in a shocking situation, we have little time to think—we just react. I saw that when the soldiers experienced fear during the Revolution."

Davie walked to his desk and sat down. "Oh, I understand that someone set John Hamilton free when the common was deserted."

"You must have stopped at Dudley's Tavern before you came to the office."

"You didn't happen to set Hamilton free, did you?"

Sam smiled as Davie nodded. A knowing grin slowly replaced the serious look on Davie's face. Sam knew what he had done was right. At least, it was right as far as Davie was concerned and Sam respected Davie's opinion.

Chapter 6

The late July weather of 1788 was unbearable. The sun beat down in unrelenting rays with such intensity that it was hard to find comfort anywhere. The long trip from Halifax to Hillsborough would be a most uncomfortable one for the delegates to the State Convention. Davie had expressed his hopes that enough support could be mustered at the convention to ratify the new Consitution, but was sure the forces of Willie Jones would present powerful opposition to any effort the Federalists delegates would make for ratification.

Since Davie's return to Halifax from the Constitutional Convention in Philadelphia, Sam had spent many hours with him in the office and had learned much about how leaders from other states regarded the new plan of government. Sam understood that there were those who felt the new nation was now maturing, and, indeed had taken its first step with the creation of the Constitution. However, there were some that felt the delegates had over-stepped their authority when they recommended the Articles of Confederation be set aside for a completely new Constitution. Many agreed that the sole purpose of the meeting in Philadelphia was to revise the old Articles. Now a bold step had been taken, and the new plan was being put before the thirteen states for approval.

The controversy over adoption was raging throughout the land, and the tension could be felt in Halifax. Willie Jones had made everybody in the state aware of his opposition to ratification, while William R. Davie strongly voiced his opinion that it should be adopted. Sam thought of the talks he had with Davie about Alexander Hamilton, who was leading the Federalists and Thomas Jefferson, who now was the leader of the Anti-Federalists. Both leaders had expressed their deep feelings about the new national government. It seemed that both men wanted what was best for the country, but differed in the way the new government should be shaped in its creation. From all Sam had heard, Alexander Hamilton thought the common people should not share in the government in the same way as the wealthy landowners or the well educated. He seemed opposed to a democratic form of government. Perhaps he had not yet come to trust the people and probably would never trust them until they become more enlightened. He apparently believed that a democracy would not function unless the people themselves were better prepared. Jefferson, on the other hand, felt the people were the government and the authority rested with the voice of the masses. With all the differences that now existed among the leaders, it was surprising to Sam that the summer of 1787 had produced any Constitution at all. There were certainly more differences of opinions at that meeting in Philadelphia than now existed between these two parties.

However, people were now aware of a three-department plan of government that was to be made of a legislature, an executive, and a judiciary.

Davie had done much to get the copies of the new Constitution before the people in North Carolina. It was being discussed across the state in almost every conceivable manner. In Halifax, it had taken precedent over such topics as cockfights, horse races, and backgammon or even the local gossip. People on the town common huddled in groups to gain a better understanding of the new plan. The taverns were filled with men who made remarks and sometimes became too violent in expressing their opinions. Discussions were taking place everywhere a speaker and a listener convened. The alehouse, the billiard halls, the boarding houses, the church, the supper table gave men and women the opportunity to express their ideas.

There were stories that Anti-federalists had hung leaders of the Federalists in effigy, and in other places, the very opposite had taken place. The great controversy in North Carolina, in Sam's opinion, was just how the state would share the authority in its relationship with the new National Government. Many Anti-Federalists feared the federal government would take away any authority that now resided with the state. There was great concern that a declaration of civil and religious liberties be a part of the new Constitution before ratification. These liberties should be put in the form of a Bill of Rights and this should be a part of the Constitution. The Federalists looked to the new plan as reverently as a preacher looked to his Bible. The Constitution would insure protection of property, control the currency and promote the welfare of the states according to each state's needs. It would also serve as the great source of authority and would make the nation strong enough to deal with riots and unrest. Sam thought of Shay's Rebellion that had taken place in Massachusetts just this past February. There were only ten men killed in the fight but it was a good example of the weakness of the government set up under the Articles of Confederation. Throughout the land people who did not feel secure became even more fearful. Sam could readily see the need for a stronger national government.

When Sam considered the two political parties and how each philosophy related to the new plan, he felt confident that both parties were right in their basic ideas—but there were many ramifications that would soon have to be reconciled.

Sam felt that he, like the great nation, was beginning to see some plan developing for his life. His relationship with Jessica had grown since that first talk. If anything was certain, it was that they had some basic values that were compatible. There was understanding and there was trust between the two. Lately, he had begun to assume that Jessica would be available whenever he called on her and he had not been disappointed.

Now in the spring of 1788, the April weather was perfect for fishing. It was Saturday, and Sam had the day off. He had convinced Jessica that it would be a perfect day. Jessica had a seventeen-year-old girl helping her but did not feel free to leave her in charge, especially on Saturday. Jessica had looked for someone for a week before Mrs. Eelbeck finally said that she was available and would keep the shop although she had at first been reluctant to offer her help since she was having Christopher Dudley over. She said she wanted to prepare something special for her guest, and if she closed the shop at five, there would be plenty of time. Dudley wasn't coming until seven.

Jessica had told Sam about Mrs. Eelbeck wanting to prepare something special for Dudley. Sam was quick to say, "Something special for someone special."

Now, in the early afternoon, Jessica and Sam rode down King Street in the light carriage Sam had borrowed from Davie. People in wagons, carriages, and gigs and on horseback met them and nodded. Several men along the street seemed to admire the carriage and smiled as if they were complimenting Sam for owning such fine property. The carriage was kept at Martin's Livery for Davie's use, but was seldom taken outside the barn. Since Davie had a handsome carriage at his own stable, he rarely ever hitched a horse to the one Sam was now driving. Davie had told Sam on several occasions that the carriage was his to use whenever he needed it. It was a light, one-horse carriage with two seats. Sam and Jessica sat up front and just behind them on the floorboards was a large picnic basket that Jessica had prepared. Sam had bought along two fishing poles and has spent the morning finding some worms for bait. There was also a bottle of Madeira that Dudley had graciously given for the occasion.

Jessica smiled and Sam felt warm and responsive. Jessica was not the most beautiful girl that Sam had ever seen; yet there was a gentle, kind look that always seemed a part of her countenance. Her pale blue eyes were the same as the summer sky, her lips were full and her cheeks had a faint tint of color. Her blonde curls danced about her head as the carriage moved along the road. Jessica had the respect of all the gentlewomen and gentlemen in Halifax. She had come to be regarded as a competent businesswoman who could bargain with the best. She had realized early in her business career that men did not favor women when it came to the power of the dollar, so, she had learned to be frugal and shrewd. Her business had become prosperous, and the quality of her goods caused even members of the aristocracy to venture her way. When these most favored people started to filter into her shop, Jessica knew that her shop was accepted as a reputable establishment, and would so be treated by her customers.

Strange Wind from the Roanoke

After passing through the residential section, they approached the Quanky Creek Bridge, which spanned a deep ravine. Sam pulled right on the reins and turned onto a road that led to Willie Jones' plantation. He let his horse walk and was in no hurry. There was plenty of time and it was too hot to be rushed. Now, the road was covered with shade from the trees that grew above the sylvan tunnel. Thin shafts of sunlight penetrated the thick foliage and darted among the shadows along the road.

Jessica looked at Sam as they rode along the shaded lane. His light blue shirt was rolled up at the sleeve, and his faded blue britches came to his knees. His old shoes were without buckles, and his purple socks had been washed to a discolored blue. He was wearing clothes that would not be suitable for any other occasion. Jessica found an old riding habit she had not worn for years and thought the light tan outfit would be just the thing to wear on this excursion at Quanky Creek.

Sam and Jessica were the only two travelers along the shaded sylvan road. There was an imperturbable stillness that was broken only by the sound of the turning wheels of the carriage and the redundant clopping of the horse's hooves and the spoken words.

"Mrs. Eelbeck said you've changed these last few weeks, Sam." Jessica stole a quick glance at Sam, which betrayed her deep concern.

"Well, I suppose nobody ever stays the same. Do you think I've changed?" Sam sounded interested.

"I can say that I've noticed you seem more alive. You used to look as if you'd lost your best friend."

"Memories linger longer when one tries to hold on too tightly to the past. I suppose I've been looking at life differently these past few weeks."

"In what way, Sam?"

"When I spend more time thinking about the present and the future than I do on the past, that's a sign of improvement—wouldn't you say?"

"I would definitely say that is an improvement provided your thoughts of the present and future are positive and you have good priorities. Tell me about your thoughts."

Sam began to feel a bit uncomfortable. "I think there's still hope for me. I'm not yet thirty years old, and my mother used to say that a man does not reach maturity until he is thirty-five. You see, I still have time."

"Have you decided to stay on with Mr. Davie at the law office?"

"I've learned a great deal about law since I've been there and I've been saving my money. I just might go to Princeton in a few years. Davie says he can get me in—that is, if I'm certain I want to go."

"I've been hearing that Davie is working hard to start a University here in North Carolina."

"It's his pet project. He is always coming back to the idea even when there is so much to be done with the ratifying of the Constitution."

"I think you'd be a good lawyer, Sam."

"I knew you'd say that. You know, I've come to understand the way you think, Jessica. I can almost tell what you're going to say before you say it."

"Then I'd better be careful what I think when I'm with you." Jessica seemed flattered by Sam's statement. "One day I just might say something or do something that will cause you to take back what you've just said, Sam Pickett."

"Jessica, I can tell you this—I've not been bored with your company even when you are silent." Sam was not prepared for the seriousness of the moment. It was as if the conversation was leading to a conclusion for which he was not prepared.

"I'm glad, Sam. I shall never be so presumptuous as to want our relationship to be any other way."

Up ahead and to the left of the main road was a turnoff that led to Quanky Creek. When Sam turned onto the side road, thick grass grew where the wheels of the carriage touched the ground and tall weeds brushed the floorboard of the carriage.

"No one uses this road anymore and this is about as far as we can go with the carriage. We'll have to walk the rest of the way," said Sam as he stepped down. He pushed back some brush and walked to the horse, untied a lead rein, and attached it to a small sweetgum tree. He came around to Jessica's side and held out his hand. Jessica stepped down.

Strange Wind from the Roanoke

Jessica smiled and Sam smiled back as he helped her down. For a brief moment they were close and the touching of her hand stirred Sam. He felt a strong need to hold her closer.

I left some slack in the rein so the horse can graze while we're gone," said Sam, for want of something better to say.

"You take the basket and the poles and the worms. I'll get the blanket," said Jessica as she handed him his share of the load.

After walking along the narrow footpath for about fifty yards, they came to a cliff. Down below about one hundred feet was the spot that Sam had remembered from his youth. Sam pointed to the creek below. "You see that log that spans the creek?"

Jessica nodded.

"That's where we want to get to."

"How can we get down there from up here?"

"We'll have to go along this cliff. There's a place just beyond those trees where we can climb down." Sam pointed to his left.

Soon they were carefully inching their way down the steep incline toward the bank of Quanky Creek. When they finally reached the spot that Sam had pointed out, Jessica looked back toward the cliff. "It doesn't look as steep from down here as it did from up there."

"You're just seeing the same thing—from a different point of view. Sometimes that can make all the difference in the world," said Sam. He thought of the Constitution —and William R. Davie—Willie Jones—and then he thought that the idea also applied to himself.

"Now don't start telling me you knew I was going to say that," said Jessica as she unfolded the blanket.

"I'll have to admit I was thinking the same thing."

Sam took the bottle of Madeira from the basket, tied a rawhide cord to the neck and lowered in into the cool water. He tied the other end of the cord securely to a bush on the bank. He reached for the fishing poles and worms. "I'm going to bait these two poles. You can get the food ready. I'll leave one pole here for you—I'm going out on the log. That's where I used to catch all my fish."

With these instructions, Sam walked a short distance and carefully made his way along the fallen log to the center of the creek.

Jessica watched Sam for a minute, picked up her pole and tossed the bait into the water. She had only begun to unpack the basket when Sam let out a loud yell—"Jessica—I've got a bite."

Jessica looked up just in time to see Sam pull in a large perch. Sam steadied himself on the log and took the fish from the hook. He walked along the log back to the bank and took his knife to cut a small forked branch. He sharpened the end of the branch and quickly pushed it through the gill of the fish. He then stuck the sharp end of the branch into the bank. The fish fluttered about and then seemed to surrender as it settled in the water.

Sam had been so concerned with his catch he had not noticed that Jessica was now out on the log and had tossed her bait in the same spot where he had caught his fish.

Just as he looked up, he saw Jessica's cork bob up and down and then it went out of sight.

"Something has my bait, Sam." Jessica pulled on the bent pole. She lost her balance and—before Sam could tell her to hold on to the log, she was falling headfirst into the water. Sam shook off his shoes and jumped into the shallow water. He swam quickly to Jessica. She was frantically trying to stay afloat when he reached out to her.

"I can't swim, Sam. I can't swim!"

Sam grabbed her and pulled her toward the bank. He lifted her in his arms as he neared the water's edge. She clung to him like a leech. He tried to let her down, but she would not let go. He squatted on the blanket and let her down gently. He let her recline on the blanket and brushed the blonde hair from her face. There was a frightened look in her eyes, and Sam felt a strong desire to hold her close. He leaned forward and kissed her tenderly on the cheek and Jessica responded to his touch. Without hesitation, Sam was kissing her waiting lips as he held her close. The feeling that came with the embrace revived old desires that could only come with one who was truly loved. There was something in her touch that Sam had not expected—something that stirred his blood and awakened feeling he thought would be dormant for the rest of his life. It was his first such embrace since he had last held Josie. His emotions were now stronger than his will, and Sam realized for the first time since Josie's death— that there was alive within his very being the desire to share his love with another. He looked longingly at the closed eyes of Jessica as she turned her face to him. There was no longer the tension and the fear— only the wonder of the moment. Sam pressed his lips to hers once more. He closed his eyes and was oblivious to all the sounds of the woods. Her tender embrace—made him feel safe and at peace.

Strange Wind from the Roanoke

Sam somehow felt suspended in time and space as his thoughts returned to the past.

"Josie—oh——Josie." Sam was suspended in time and feeling the wonder.

Jessica pushed Sam back and there was a startled look on her face.

"What's wrong?" Sam did not seem to be aware of what he had said.

"Josie! That's what's wrong. You called me JOSIE. Sam, you called me Josie!"

"I'm sorry, Jessica."

"It's not the first time you've called me by her name. I told myself it didn't matter when you were sick. I can't fool myself any longer."

"Jessica, I don't know what you're talking about."

"That night when your fever was high I spent the night in your bed. I knew how much you loved Josie. I pretended to be her."

"I give you my word, Jessica. I don't remember what happened that night."

"I know, Sam. You have no reason to remember. The circumstances are quite different now. You are fully aware of what you're doing."

"Do you feel that I took advantage of you?"

"No, Sam. I knew what I was doing. You were the one who was being deceived. I loved you long before I came to your room that night you were sick. I can't count the time I've stood at the window of my shop and watched you pass on your way to and from Davie's Office—even before that—I remember the day you came to warn us that Cornwallis was coming—I think I have loved you from that first time I saw you."

Chapter 7

"Jessica, what are we to do?" Sam reached out to her but Jessica stopped him.

"I love you, Sam. Now you know that—but I realize that no one can take Josie's place. Not now, anyway—and I'm not willing to wait because there just may not ever be a time when you are free of the memory of her."

"I can't promise you anything, Jessica."

"Perhaps it would be better if we stop seeing each other for a while." Jessica seemed to think they needed some time to think about the relationship.

"I can't promise anyone that I'll ever love again the way I loved Josie. You must know how I feel about you, Jessica."

"That's not enough, Sam. The love that you are offering is not complete love. Memories of Josie are still too much with you."

"I understand, Jessica. I hope this doesn't mean that we can't continue to see each other and be friends."

"I see no reason why we can't be friends, Sam."

Suddenly the moment was shattered. Sam and Jessica were startled at the sound of a high-pitched screechy voice.

"HEY, YA'LL LOST A FISHIN' POLE?"

Strange Wind from the Roanoke

Sam looked up at the specter. The glaring sun was directly behind the being and she looked like an apparition. Jessica shaded her eyes to see who had invaded their privacy. She seemed glad to see that it was the old swamp woman, Looney Oney, who looked down on them.

"Ah wah down stream when ah seen this pole floatin' along just-a-bobbin'- up and down. I chunked mah line to the pole and pulled it to the bank." She reached down and held up a black catfish the length of her arm. "Dis wah on the end of the line."

Sam stood up and took the catfish from Looney Oney and put it with the other fish.

"You catching anything down stream, Oney?" Sam asked as he returned to the blanket.

"Just utter people's fishin' poles. Ah ain't had a bite since Ah got heah. Ah come to fish and can't catch nothing, and here ya'll are layin' back lack you didn't come to fish at tall and ya'll done hung a big catfish."

"We were just getting ready to have a picnic," said Jessica.

"Oh, yeah! Looked lack ya'll was having it when Ah come up." Oney looked at them slyly indicating that she knew better.

"You still staying in that cabin upstream, Oney?" asked Sam as he looked closely at the old woman. Her presence changed the atmosphere. It was as if there was something more than Looney Oney that had become a part of the scene.

Looney Oney squatted on the ground next to the blanket.

"Been livin' heah for over fifteen years. Ah gits to town now and then. Mr. Willie furnishes me wid stuff if Ah goes to his door. Ah'm most partial to Mrs. Eelbeck. She helps me when Ah'm in need. Now, Ah'm usually in need but Mrs. Eelbeck needs Oney, too. Mr. Dudley gives me leavins from his kitchen. Ah thank that's the last time Ah saw you Sam Pickett. When Jesse Turner tried to shame me. I understand he was SHAMED when he was put in that cell wid Mr. Harry Bedlow."

"I remember that time." Sam nodded as he recalled the prophecy.

"Oney don't need nothin' but good friends, some beeswax to make my candles and a little money now and then."

"With friends like that, what do you need money for, Oney?" asked Sam.

""Oney takes a little wine or ale when she's a mind to." Oney smiled, showing a space where two of her upper teeth were missing. "It helps to make mah spirits come alive. You know, Ah'm accustomed to having spirits of mah own."

Oney's bronze skin told of her mixed ancestry and those muddy eyes revealed nothing of her past. Sam could understand why some people speculated about her.

Jessica spread the food and handed Oney a chicken leg and a biscuit.

Sam pulled the bottle of Madeira from the creek and poured some of the cool wine into two mugs that Jessica handed him from the basket.

"Now, Oney, I know how you talk about the weird sights and sounds you see and hear in the swamps—and how you make all kinds of prophecies when you come to town. So, will you tell me what it is you see for me?" Sam felt fatwitted even as he asked the question.

Looney Oney stood and looked down at Sam with an inquisitive stare. Much the same as when a dog hears a strange sound. "You mean you rilly wants to know what I see that is befo' you?"

"Only if it's good," said Sam exchanging a smile with Jessica.

"You want to know what it is dat 'll brang you happiness. You do know dat what dat word means depends on who's doing the wantin'", Oney looked inquiringly at Sam, then continued.

"You'll haft to give me some object that is yourn—Ah got to touch somethin' that belongs." Oney looked serious and her whole demeanor changed.

"I'll give you the rest of this wine. Will that serve your need?" Sam handed the bottle to Oney.

"Now, dat'll do just fine. Some spirits can be brought up just after some spirits goes down." Oney lifted the bottle and took a deep swallow. She closed her eyes and licked her lips and looked as if she were in a trance.

"There is—a whirling wind—a strange gust of wind—dat will come to you—wind will brang change—-it be strange—and brang change—it be strange —and it brang change." Oney chanted these words and then sank slowly to the ground. She shook her head from side to side and regained her presence of mind. Sam did not know if Jessica sensed it or if it was just his imagination but there seemed

Strange Wind from the Roanoke

some kind of omniscience now that was not present before Oney had joined them.

Sam looked at Jessica who seemed completely absorbed by all that Looney Oney had said. "I hope the wind brings good times for all of us, Oney. Look, I want you to forget you saw Jessica and me here today. I can imagine what it will sound like when you start telling people about the way you caught that big catfish."

"Now, you know Ah wouldn't tell a soul. Not now, naw, Suh." Oney looked at the label on the bottle as if she were reading it.

"That's imported wine, Oney. Don't imagine you've ever tasted wine like that before. Don't get use to the taste," warned Sam.

Oney took the dark bottle to her lips. When she turned the bottle down she smacked her lips. "Ummmmmm—hummmmm. Best Ah ever tasted. Oney don't git too much important wine. Well, Ah got to git back to mah fishin' and Ah knows you two have to git back to whatever it is you got to git back to."

"Don't forget what I told you Oney," reminded Sam.

"How am Ah to remember when you told me to forgit. Ah have already forgot what you told me not to remember". Oney turned the half-empty bottle up to the sun "Ah might not catch no fish here today, but Ah don't much care. Ah hopes the spirits will be good to both of you." She pressed the bottle to her chest. "Ah knows dey goin' to be good to me. Oh, tell Mrs. Eelbeck that Ah'm coming to town later. I'll stop by to see if she wants me to skin that catfish."

"I'll tell her but don't you say anything about how you helped to catch it."

Jessica looked at Sam and they both laughed as Oney disappeared in the brush.

Sam wondered just how Oney would interpret his strange dream of Josie's funeral. There was an explanation—he knew that. He decided that he would seek her counsel if the dream continued to plague him.

Sam and Jessica finished the food and fished until the sun was low. Soon they had a nice catch of perch to put with the big catfish. When they had climbed the steep incline, they stopped at the top of the cliff and looked back at the creek below. Looney Oney was strolling along a path that led upstream to her cabin. She was singing at the top of her screechy voice. The sounds reverberated along the walls of the cliff and floated about the trees. Birds took to wing and there was the sound of animals scurrying about in the dense undergrowth.

"I think the spirits have got to her," said Sam.

"I only got a glimpse of her as she was going along the path. She looked as if she might be one of them," agreed Jessica.

It was almost five o'clock when they returned to the Boarding House. Mrs. Eelbeck took one look at the catfish and thought a "catfish muddle" would be just the thing for her boarders. Sam had heard Dudley talk about the way Mrs. Eelbeck could make a "catfish muddle". She would put the fish in with the parsley, onions and potatoes. While it was slowly cooking, she would add some garlic and other ingredients that gave her "catfish muddle" that special flavor. Dudley would be pleased to sit at a bowl later on when he came to call.

Sam and Jessica did not mention just how the fish was caught. If the boarders knew that Looney Oney played any part in the catch—then—they might be reluctant to partake of the meal. Sam knew that Christopher Dudley was superstitious enough to think the catfish had been conjured up out of the water without any bait ever being used. He was one man who would not even venture to call Oney "Looney".

The next day Reverend Ford came by the office and talked at great length about the tense feeling that existed among the members of his congregation. There were those who spoke to Reverend Ford in confidence regarding their loyalty to Willie Jones and the Anti-Federalists. Still, others were as equally devoted to William R. Davie and the Federalists. Reverend Ford seemed to feel that his church was no longer large enough for these two groups to meet under the same roof. He seemed concerned about the welfare of all those who were still in bondage. He said he didn't understand how the slaves could be counted as three-fifths for tax purposes and three-fifths for population to determine the seats in the House of Representatives. He was unable to give any kind of suggestion as to the solution but he had a deep concern that it would be a while before any of the great plantation owners would be willing to set the slaves free. The Reverend Ford was concerned about where the slaves would go and who would care for them if they were set free. Then, he decided that the future welfare of the slaves would be left to those who would be in charge of making the laws. Just before he left the office, the Reverend urged Sam to survey some more lots at the back of the cemetery. Several families

Strange Wind from the Roanoke

had requested lots and none were available. Sam promised that he would see to it just as soon as he had some free time.

Sam had been so involved with his work at the office he had little time for anything other than the work that was demanded of him. Now and then, when there was a brief lapse in his schedule, thoughts of Jessica returned to tease his mind.

After considering the situation at some length, he decided to move from Mrs. Eelbeck's Boarding House and take a room at Dudley's Tavern. Dudley was always willing for Sam to come and stay at the Tavern. He told Mrs. Eelbeck that it was two blocks closer to the office and Dudley had offered him the spare room.

Mrs. Eelbeck sensed that there was some other reason and Sam was finally compelled to give her the logical explanation.

"I just want to be sure of what I'm doing. I don't think I'm ready for a serious relationship." Sam did not know why but he sounded almost apologetic.

"I can understand that. It's better to be sure before you make any kind of commitment."

"I just need some time to see just how much Jessica means to me, I suppose."

Mrs. Eelbeck nodded. "That's the only way—sometimes. You two stop seeing each other for a while—make new acquaintances. It'll do both of you good. Then, you two can determine how you feel about each other. The course of true love never did run smooth."

"When you see Jessica, will you tell her that I've taken a room at Dudley's?"

"I'll talk with her. I'm sure she'll want to know your reason for leaving." Mrs. Eelbeck reluctantly agreed.

In the coming weeks Sam saw Jessica in passing and was polite to her but did not ask her out or even get involved in any lengthy conversation. Their relationship was one which close friends enjoy and Sam sincerely felt that Jessica was one of the dearest friends he had in Halifax.

Sam did not recall the exact date but it was some time in the middle of June that a young printer named Thomas Fargo moved to Halifax. He set up a shop in the basement of Martin's Tavern. Fargo was a handsome young man of twenty-six with a skill at printing far beyond his years.

Fargo was not in Halifax long before he started taking his meals at Mrs. Eelbeck's Boarding House. Since Sam continued eating there, he had the opportunity to make Fargo's acquaintance. Sam quickly spoke to him regarding William R. Davie's need for a printer.

Soon Davie employed the master printer to print pamphlets, petitions and copies of the Constitution. Fargo's work was of the finest quality and everybody became impressed with the young man. Davie came to rely on him for all his printing needs.

Tom Fargo was in Halifax no more than a week when he moved to take the room that Sam had vacated at the Boarding House. It was there that he first met Jessica and started what Sam considered to be a hasty relationship. Lately he had seen the two at the common. They seemed always to be enjoying each other's company. On one occasion, Jessica had attended a party at John Baptiste Ashe's home and the printer had accompanied her. Dudley had made a special trip to the office to bring that message.

Sam on the other hand, had not thought of any other girl and really wondered if he had been too hasty to act when he had agreed with Jessica that they should stop seeing each other. Whatever happiness Jessica shared with Tom Fargo could be directly attributed to none other than Sam Pickett. He knew that. What Sam couldn't determine was whether Jessica was pretending to enjoy herself or if she really was finding Tom Fargo that attractive. "The course of true love never did run smooth," echoed in Sam's mind as he remembered the conversation with Mrs. Eelbeck.

In the course of all that was happening, there was still time for the annual Fourth of July LIBERTY BALL that was celebrated at Martin's Tavern. Plans had been made for the occasion and it was to be attended by all the local people and their guest. Many visitors were beginning to arrive at the home of: Willie Jones, Allen Jones, John Ashe and Benjamin McCullen. Letters were written to friends, well in advance, and many were now finding places at private homes and at the inns. Young ladies visited close friends, and young men thought this a most opportune occasion to meet the young ladies. Sam thought the ball had grown too large and was convinced that he was right when the Ball Committee announced that all of Market Street and the town common would be used for the occasion. Members of the Ball Committee became apprehensive and somewhat overwhelmed at all the new faces that appeared in Halifax three days prior to the Fourth of July celebration.

Committees had been formed to handle all the different aspects of the gala event. A beverage committee to provide all the liquid refreshments, a food committee had delegated cooking duties to the ladies, an entertainment committee had secured a five piece string band from Scotland Neck, a decorating committee had continuously worked in the Ball Room at Martin's Tavern for the past two weeks—all this preparation bespoke the great effort that was necessary to insure a successful LIBERTY BALL.

Sam was closing the front door of the law office that first day of July, when Benjamin McCullen came up the walk. He was dressed in a handsome white shirt with a light blue silk britches. His appearance was much different from what Sam remembered when he had seen McCullen at the gaol. He now looked sophisticated and dressed like a gentleman. Today he looked like the proud owner of the McCullen Plantation.

"Sam, I'm glad you're still here," began McCullen as he came near.

"I'm just closing for the day. Did you want to see Mr. Davie?"

"No, Sam. I came to see you."

"Well, let's walk over to Dudley's —that's where I'm staying now."

The two walked toward Dudley's Tavern and just as they came to the town common, Benjamin McCullen asked Sam to sit with him on the wooden bench that was usually occupied by Mr. Hedgepeth.

"I left my horse across the street at Martin's Livery and I need to get back to the farm as soon as I can. You know, I don't like to be away too long at the time. It seems that the work always slows down when I'm off the land."

"You don't get to town enough, Benjamin," said Sam, noticing an uneasiness in McCullen's manner.

"Sam, we have guests at our house," said McCullen, getting immediately to the purpose of his visit. "That's the reason I want to talk with you. They're old friends, and they'll be staying all next week. Now, there's a young lady involved. She especially wants to come to the LIBERTY BALL. When we started talking about it, I thought of you immediately. She needs an escort, Sam."

"I suppose I'm available. I'd better check my social calendar just to make sure I haven't promised myself to any other fortunate young lady," said Sam smiling.

"In that case, I assume you accept."

"Might I ask the name of the young lady?"

"I would rather you wouldn't Sam. Let me say this, you will not be disappointed. I'll stake my whole tobacco crop on it."

"Now wait—I don't know that I like this arrangement."

"You'll be more than delighted when you've seen her. She'll be one of the most beautiful young ladies at the ball. I give you my word, Sam."

"You make it hard for me to refuse."

"You come on out about six o'clock and we'll come to the ball in my carriage."

"I shall look forward to the fourth," said Sam. He shook hands with McCullen as if to seal the bargain.

"Wear your finest clothes, Sam. I've already seen her gown, and you don't want to be caught wanting," said McCullen, looking back to Sam as he walked toward the livery stable.

"I have only one dress suit and it's my finest," yelled Sam, waving to McCullen.

Sam anticipated the LIBERTY BALL and made all kinds of preparations in advance. He even walked across the street from Dudley's to check on the decorations just to make sure that everything was progressing on schedule. Sam talked at great length with Christopher Dudley about the ball. Dudley said that Mrs. Eelbeck would have the pleasure of his company, and that they were walking from the Boarding House with Mr. Tom Fargo and Miss Jessica Jackson.

When Dudley asked Sam whom he was escorting, Sam truthfully told him that he was not aware of her name. Then, Dudley had remarked that, "they're the kind you have to watch. You remember that farm girl at the church social? Suppose it turns out to be her—now that would serve you right. That would be something to behold."

What Dudley said stayed on Sam's mind for the next two days.

"McCullen wouldn't do anything like that—would he?" Sam had spoken these words aloud several times whenever he considered how little he knew about the real character of Benjamin McCullen.

Strange Wind from the Roanoke

On the day of the ball, Sam took his change of clothes and neatly folded his dark brown knee britches, his white laced ruffled shirt, his embroidered waistcoat, and open front dress coat, then closed his valise. He wore his buckled shoes, and would only have to wipe the road dust from them when he prepared to leave McCullen's for the ball.

He arrived at the McCullen Plantation shortly after six o'clock and was met at the door by a bronze-skinned girl. who immediately led him to the large family room just down the hall. As they approached the large room, the girl took Sam's valise and told him his clothes would be laid out in the guestroom, which was to the left of the stairs.

The family room that Sam entered was decorated in many shades of blue. Benjamin McCullen walked to Sam and welcomed him.

"Come on in, Sam. This is Mr. Archibald Hamilton," said McCullen as he pushed a chair back for him.

"Oh, yes, Sir. I remember you had a store in New Bern before the war. You're the brother of my father -in-law—John Hamilton. Sam noticed the great resemblance as he extended his hand.

"You have a great memory, Sam. It's been over thirteen years. I remember John came to New Bern when he left Halifax. I never shared my bothers' loyalties. So, he stayed at my home for only a brief time."

"I remember the night John Hamilton and his family left Halifax. I was there that night," said Sam.

"We're on our way back to Boston. I have some letters of credit that I want to take to John. Jenny has heard so much about the LIBERTY BALL we could not pass this way without making good the invitation that Rebecca McCullen sent her."

"He was here last year on some business with Mr. William R. Davie," said Sam.

"I, too, have some business with Davie. I hope to see him tonight at the ball," said Hamilton.

"I'm sure he'll be there. In fact, I think everybody will be there," assured Sam.

Sam sat in the high-backed chair that had been offered him. Hamilton sat across from him and McCullen took the chair next to Sam.

"Sam, I hope you don't think I'm imposing on you—but Jenny has talked of nothing but this ball since we arrived. Since her mother's death, I've had to see to her wishes."

"I'm sure I'll find great pleasure in her company," said Sam.

After talking briefly about the federal Constitution and the great effort the Federalists were putting forth in North Carolina, Sam was taken to the guestroom.

"Jenny is upstairs with Rebecca; they should be down soon, Sam. You get dressed and I'll see what I can find to wear. Hamilton said he only had to get his coat." McCullen continued down the hall.

"I'll only need a few minutes," said Sam, as he turned to his left and entered the room.

His britches and shirt were laid out on the bed and his coat was hanging from an oak valet at the foot of the bed. After removing his shirt, he went to the wash basin and found fresh towels and a wash cloth. Next to the wash basin was a body length mirror where he saw his full reflection. He watched himself as he prepared for the ball. After washing himself thoroughly, he stepped closer to the mirror and brushed his hair back and tied it with a black ribbon. He then splashed some sweet smelling cologne on each cheek, stepped to the bed, and put on his best clothes. Upon looking again at the mirror, as he finished dressing, he was not at all disappointed at the image reflected there. Now he felt he was prepared to join the others.

Just as he left the guestroom, Rebecca McCullen came down the stairs.

"Hello, Sam. Listen, I haven't had the chance to thank you for your kindness to Benjamin while he was unjustly confined in that dreadful goal," said Rebecca, speaking softly as if she were sharing a secret.

"It was most convenient for me to be of assistance. I usually pass that gaol every day. The fact is—he seldom wanted anything," said Sam, quietly continuing the conversation.

"I do know Benjamin appreciated your visits, Sam. He has often spoken of those days."

"Your gown is beautiful," said Sam, noticing the long light pink gown, which was laced with dark pink ribbons at the bottom. The top of her gown was the same shade of pink as her ribbons. The sleeves were short and pushed up on her shoulders to appear puffed.

Strange Wind from the Roanoke

"It's the first chance I've had to wear it. I think it's a little tight." Rebecca tugged at the mid-section indicating the source of discomfort. She was thirty-five years old, and her dark hair was in curls. She was stout with tanned muscular arms. He brown eyes showed an excitement that was not usually there and a gardenia aroma accentuated her pleasant disposition. The aroma reminded him of Jessica. Even though the aroma of gardenia was pleasant he thought that lilac was even more pleasant.

"Jenny is on her way down. She's been preparing for the ball most of the afternoon, but don't tell her I said so."

Just as Rebecca spoke, Sam looked to the stairs and there stood Jenny. He looked quickly to Rebecca, who smiled demurely, as if she were pleased with his reaction.

At the top of the stairs stood a young lady so beautiful—so much the likeness of his own beloved Josie—that Sam took the rail of the stair for fear his legs would not support him. Her dark eyelashes, the blue of her eyes, her figure, her brown hair, and even the smile she now gave him were unbelievable characteristics of the wife that he had once adored.

She stood there momentarily and Sam only stared. A beautiful golden gown of silk covered her attractive figure. Her skirt was divided in front and a shade darker than her petticoat. The bodice was of darker gold, a color deeper than her gown. The wrist-length sleeves had pleated cuffs, which curved to fit at the bend of her arms. Long brown curls danced about her shoulders.

Then she spoke. "Hello, Sam Pickett." There was a softness in her voice that cause Sam to gasp in disbelief. Her smile was slightly sensuous, as if to hint of things to come.

As Jenny came down the stair, Sam held out his hand to her. He felt awkward and could only smile weakly as she put her hand in his.

"Jenny—Jenny—Hamilton, I know you must think me rude—but—I—I just can't believe your favor to my wife—Josie."

Jenny nodded her head. "When we were children, some of our kin used to say we were like twins," said Jenny, as they walked from the hall to the family room. There was something inviting just the way she moved. Something more than inviting—something suggestive.

Soon the men were ready and they were on their way to Halifax. Sam and Jenny sat in the back seat of the carriage behind

Benjamin and Rebecca. Mr. Archibald Hamilton followed. He had expressed his wish to leave the ball early, so he wanted to drive McCullen's gig.

Sam was glad that Mr. Hamilton followed. Somehow he felt more at ease with Hamilton not close enough to hear all he wanted to say to Jenny. As this thought came to him, he wondered what it would be that he could say to someone such as Jenny Hamilton.

Chapter 8

When Sam and his party crossed the wooden bridge at Quanky Creek they merged into a single line of carriages headed toward the town common. Benjamin McCullen sensed that there would be no hope of finding any place near Martin's Tavern to tie up his horse, so Sam suggested that they turn off on Pittsylvania Avenue, and pull in behind Mrs. Eelbeck's Boarding House. There was enough space there for the two carriages and Sam felt sure that Mrs. Eelbeck wouldn't mind if they tied up there.

Mrs. Eelbeck evidently had already left for the ball, for she was not at the Boarding House when Sam went to the door to get permission.

Soon Sam and the others joined couples who were walking down King Street. Carriages along the road were stalled and some drivers were pulling to the side of the road to leave their carriages. Some of the passengers were leaving the carriages with the understanding that this was about as close as they would get to Martin's Tavern. The walk from King Street was only one block.

Sam thought of the large gathering he had seen at the church social, but nothing he had ever seen could compare with the elegance and glamour that were expected and indeed essential to such an occasion as the LIBERTY BALL.

It was almost eight o'clock by the time the party reached the corner of Market Street. The town common was filled with people who were politely talking and renewing acquaintances. There was a thickening of the crowd as they moved along Market Street towards Martin's Tavern. They meandered through the crowd, nudging and apologizing as they neared the front door of the tavern.

Once inside the now converted ballroom, the party waited at the entrance until the couples ahead of them found places to sit. Sam looked about the large room and admired the results of the fine work done by the ladies of Halifax. Tables to the west end of the room, next to the bar, were laden with salads and goodies of all kinds. Beyond this table was the bar, which was now being used by some men who stood toasting their mugs filled with different kind of brandy, wine and ale.

The ladies were mingling among the early arrivals showing off their finest gowns, which were as colorful as the many shades of autumn when the sun is at its zenith. The atmosphere inside was intoxicating as odors of lilac, rose and other fragrances floated toward the newcomers. There was already a mood of gaiety, permeating the hall enhanced by the lively chirping and chattering of the ladies as they moved about the ballroom.

Gentlemen were in silk britches that buttoned at the knees. Light embroidered waistcoats were worn beneath a long coats with back splits and opened fronts. Most of the long coats had no cuffs but had buttoned splits to reveal the sleeve of the ruffled shirt. Some gentlemen were taking off the light coats and hanging them on the coat racks near the front door. Several men wore a new style of English boot which had tops turned down to show a canvas lining, but most of the men wore flat black shoes with silver buckles. The older men were wearing powdered wigs and puffed hair about the ears and frizzled bangs in front. The younger men who were fortunate have hair to style had their hair brushed back over their ears and tied in queue.

To the right of the entrance was a small table where a lady was checking the names of all that entered. Sam felt proud to know that his name was among those who were on the "Ball List". As they inched closer to the ballroom floor, Benjamin McCullen gave the names of all that were in his party. To the far end of the ballroom and directly opposite the bar was a platform where five young musicians

Strange Wind from the Roanoke

from Scotland Neck tuned their stringed instruments. At the center of the room and twenty feet above the dance floor was a large silver-coated sphere three feet in diameter. From this hub radiated streamers of silk as colorful as any rainbow Sam had ever seen. Wooden beams about ten feet above the dance floor stretched around the perimeter of the dance area and to these beams were attached the multi-colored ribbon streamers. Sam was so impressed with the decoration that McCullen had to tug at his sleeve to gain his attention.

"There's a table directly across the dance floor," said McCullen, pointing across the room.

Soon they were settled and the musicians began to play a lively minuet. Some of the young gentlemen seemed stirred by the music and immediately took the ladies to the floor. Sam was not too eager to do the minuet, and thought he would wait for a while. He considered this idea only briefly and was about to explain this to Jenny when a tall young gentleman dressed in a fine green silk suit approached the table. He walked directly to Jenny and extended his hand. "May I have the honor?"

Jenny looked at Sam.

Sam nodded, as if it would please him to see her dance.

Now sitting opposite the front door, Sam could see that other couples were arriving. Willie Jones and Mary Montfort Jones entered with John Baptiste Ashe and Elizabeth Montfort Ashe; William R. Davie and Sarah Jones Davie accompanied Allen Jones and his wife; John Alston and his wife were in the company of Nicholas Long and his wife.

Down the ballroom and to the right from where Sam sat was an area that was reserved for these families.

As soon as they were settled at their tables, servants who were present only to attend them served them different drinks.

Sam looked back to the dance floor and watched the graceful movements of Jenny as she provocatively smiled at her tall young partner. More than twenty people were moving about on the floor and the dance was just beginning.

Sam made himself satisfied to sit and watch those who stepped lightly to the sound of music. Jenny was, beyond any doubt, the center of attention. There were three lively minuets and Jenny never left the dance floor. She danced with a different partner each dance. Sam noticed several young gentlemen stood at the edge of the dance floor, waiting for the opportunity to dance with Jenny. Jenny's inviting smile seemed to encourage all the young men who looked her way.

Across the room to the left of the entrance sat Christopher Dudley and Mrs. Eelbeck—but they were alone. Sam looked back to the dance floor and soon was able to locate Jessica and Tom Fargo. Jessica was in a very beautiful blue gown that was tight at the waist and laced at the top. Her gown was revealingly low cut as were many other gowns that Sam admired when he looked about the room. Jessica's gown was no more revealing than some of the others, but he felt Jessica was being too bold.

Mr. Archibald Hamilton excused himself and walked to the bar where William R. Davie was talking to Nicholas Long and several other gentlemen. The music stopped and the dancers returned to their tables.

Just as Hamilton left the table, Benjamin McCullen quickly looked at Sam.

"Don't let Jenny stray too far from you tonight, Sam."

"Why do you say that, Benjamin?"

"Just remember what I said." McCullen had to stop the conversation before Jenny came back to the table and she was only a few feet away.

Sam had just enough time to notice Rebecca McCullen who nodded, indicating that she agreed with all that Benjamin had said.

"I thank you Miss Jenny for the dance. I shall look forward to yet another," said the tall young man as he bowed and then walked away.

The music was beginning and Sam took Jenny's hand. Benjamin and Rebecca McCullen joined them on the crowded dance floor as they stepped to the music of a waltz. Sam and Jenny dance near Jessica's table and Sam smiled. Jenny noticed the sudden change of expression on Sam's face and she, too, smiled in Jessica's direction.

When the waltz was over, Sam took Jenny's arm and they walked to Christopher Dudley's table.

"Jenny, I'd like you meet some dear friends of mine."

Dudley and Mrs. Eelbeck stood and Tom Fargo pulled Jessica's chair back so she could move around the table toward Sam and Jenny.

Strange Wind from the Roanoke

"This is Mr. Christopher Dudley, Mrs. Susanna Eelbeck—Mr. Tom Fargo and Miss Jessica Jackson." Sam turned to Jenny. "And this is Miss Jenny Hamilton."

"I am happy to know all of you. Sam has been a most gracious escort, and I really appreciate this opportunity to attend the LIBERTY BALL. I've heard so much about it. This is my first visit back here since the Revolution." Jenny squeezed Sam's arm as she spoke.

"You must be Archibald Hamilton's daughter," said Dudley.

"Why, yes, he's over at the bar, I see", said Jenny, just as if she knew where he'd be found.

"I understand that your family never left New Bern during the Revolution. I admire your father for standing up for what he believed. He's a man to look up to but John Hamilton —well there's a man who fought for the British better than any British soldier in the King's Army," said Dudley.

"The war is over, Dudley", reminded Sam, feeling a bit uneasy about the conversation.

"Would you like to join us, Sam? You and Miss Jenny?" asked Mrs. Eelbeck.

"We have a table on the other side of the room. I think I'll feel more comfortable over there, Sam," said Jenny, glancing quickly at Dudley.

"I hope you enjoy your stay in Halifax," said Jessica, smiling at Jenny.

"I am enjoying it more today than any time since I've been here. This is a grand ball," said Jenny.

She looked around the room and tugged on Sam's arm.

"The LIBERTY BALL is a great social occasion. It gives one many opportunities to meet other people," said Mrs. Eelbeck.

Jenny looked at Sam. "One does not need to look unless one is not satisfied with one's escort. Sam has been more than kind and considerate."

"It is always a great comfort to be sure of one's feelings," said Jessica, emphasizing the word "one".

Sam noticed what seemed to be a warning in Jessica's voice so he quickly changed the subject.

"Well, I see they're lighting the candles. It was beginning to get a little dark in here." Sam turned and referred to the servants who were moving from table to table lighting the candles. Two manservants were also lighting the candles in the sconces along the walls.

Suddenly everybody in the room turned toward a commotion at the bandstand where William R. Davie was standing on the platform.

"Let's get back to our table. Davie is going to speak. We'll talk with you all later. Have a good time." Sam took Jenny's arm and the two hurried to their table.

Davie began to speak before they were seated.

"Ladies and gentlemen, I have been asked to speak to you about a matter that is of great concern to all of us. Sarah, as you all know, is in charge of the entertainment committee. I shall not attempt to entertain you, but I do wish to make all of you aware of the great meaning of this Fourth of July celebration. Tonight we are indeed fortunate to be celebrating a momentous day in our your history. This day marks the birth of this nation. For all of us, who struggled through the great revolution, there must be a greater reward than what we have thus far realized. The greatness that can come will be ours only if we deserve it. As of this time we still remain outside the United States of America, and will remain in this awkward state unless we ratify the Constitution and join with the other states to form a more perfect union. We have not been represented in the first Congress—our vessels are considered alien vessels when we trade with states along the coast. Most of the hard money we are fortunate enough to acquire comes from trade with other states. I personally do not like the idea that only North Carolina and Rhode Island now remain outside the union. I have great hopes that the next convention in Fayetteville will be more favorable and support this great plan for our country. I urge all of you to support this effort with all your strength. Thank you. Now enjoy yourselves."

There was a great round of applause as Davie stepped down. As the crowd stood, Willie Jones walked quickly to the platform. He held his hands up and the crowd responded with silence.

"I want to thank all of you for the interest you have in Mary's health. She is expecting any day now and we both are anxious to find out if it is a boy or a girl. I am sure she'll be wanting all of you to come by to see the child. That is not the reason I have come to this stage tonight. All of you here know how I have voted in the past regarding the adoption of this new plan of government. I have recently been accused of making different slanderous remarks regarding the character of Mr. William R. Davie, and even the character of George Washington. Tonight, I want to publicly state that I have nothing but the highest esteem for Mr. Davie and Mr. Washington. As for Mr. Davie, I regard him as a personal friend and a strong political leader in this state and even in this nation. Perhaps the convention in Fayetteville will adopt the new Constitution, and if that be the case, I shall obey the laws that are set forth to guide us in our conduct. Until that day comes, I shall continue to fight for those freedoms that guarantee liberties to the people. I do feel that this is now possible since Mr. James Madison has introduced a bill of rights. I usually leave all the speech making to my fellow politicians, but since some man who refused to sign his name has questioned my character—I feel it is my duty to speak to all of you here. Thank you."

Willie Jones walked back to his table where Davie stood with his hand outstretched. There was much backslapping and loud congratulations as he joined the group. If there was any animosity between these two gentlemen, there was no evidence of it—not at the LIBERTY BALL.

There was a rest break for the members of the band, which signified the ball had reached its halfway period. People began to meander to the tables to get refreshments. Sam thought this would be a good time for them to mingle. Jenny had complained about the heat earlier, and Sam had suggested that they might find it more comfortable outside. Jenny had also expressed an interest to see all that was going on at the town common.

Just as they stepped outside Martin's Tavern, it became apparent that the commoners had congregated on the town common. Lanterns now lighted the area. Sam and Jenny hurried toward the sound of a lively fiddle that was coming from the corner of King and Market. Standing atop a wagon, a small man moved up and down the length of the wagon while dancers moved to the music of his fiddle. "It's the Virginia Reel," shouted Jenny, as she encouraged Sam to hurry along.

After they had moved through the crowd that surrounded the common, they could see a large circle of dancing men and women who shouted and yelled as if they were dancing on a bed of coals.

"Everybody here seems to be having fun. The people inside don't know how to enjoy themselves," said Jenny. There was excitement in her eyes.

Almost like a magnet Jenny seemed drawn to the crowd, and before Sam had time to say a word, they were moving among the dancers, who were dancing about in a circle—changing partners and moving again. As Sam danced from one partner to another, he became aware of the strong smell of corn liquor that seemed to be a part of all that was making the crowd so lively. Soon the music stopped and Sam looked about the crowd for Jenny. She was nowhere to be seen. Sam hurried through the crowd toward the wagon where the fiddler stood. He thought Jenny could have returned to where they had been standing before they were separated.

When he came to where the fiddler stood, Sam jumped on the wagon to get a better view. From where he stood, he could see clearly over the town common—but he did not see Jenny. The fiddler started another lively tune and began moving. The dancers responded to the rhythm of the music. Sam looked closely at more than thirty people to see if Jenny was among the dancers. She was not there. Then it dawned on him that Jenny might have thought that he had gone back to the ballroom. He jumped down from the wagon and made his way through the crowd.

After entering the ballroom, Sam walked quickly to Benjamin McCullen, who was standing near the bar with Allen Jones.

"Where's Jenny, Sam?" McCullen was quick to ask, as he looked around the ballroom.

"I don't know. I thought maybe she came back here. We were at the common and I lost her in the crowd."

"Are you sure she didn't lose you?"

"What do you mean?"

"Well, from all I can understand, she has a way of misbehaving at times."

"She's probably still at the common. I'd better go back out there and find her."

"If you don't find her soon, come back here for me," said McCullen, as Sam hurried from the room.

When he reached the town common, Sam looked among the many faces. He made a complete circle at the common and then returned to Market Street. He was about ready to go back to the

Strange Wind from the Roanoke

ballroom for Benjamin McCullen when he noticed several men going toward Martin's Livery. He turned to a short, stubby fellow whose wig was cocked and too large for his small head.

"What's going on at the stable?"

"THE LIVERY BALL. Ain't cha-heard?"

"The Livery Ball!" echoed Sam.

"Thash where we go to be liverated. A whole wagon load of corn liquor was dilibered about an hour ago. They got a hay loft full of spirits. Ah jist come from over there. You'd better hurry if you want to be delibered—liverated—ah—what—ah mean is if you want a drank of corn liquor."

Sam thanked the delivered man whose spirit was so mixed with corn liquor that his tongue created words as mixed in meaning as his thoughts.

Since he had looked every place he knew to look, Sam thought he just might check the stables. The short lane leading to the stables had a white rail fence on each side and several couples leaned against it. These lovers were oblivious to the presence of any person other than the one they were clinging to. Just as he approached the large barn, he saw Jesse Turner coming through the opening of the sliding doors. He was holding Jenny Hamilton close and she seemed to have trouble putting one foot in front of the other. Both Jesse and Jenny appeared to depend on each other for any kind of movement. Sam hurried towards the barn.

"What's going on here, Jesse?" Sam stood directly in Jesse's path.

"Aw, we're jest havin' some fun at the LIVERY BALL. Dish little Hamilton girl sed she was thirsty, so Ah helped her revive her spirits, dash all," said the thick-tongued Turner.

Jenny threw back her head. "Hello, Sam Pickett. Did you get lost or wash it me."

"Come on with me, Jenny. I'm going to take you to Mrs. Eelbeck's Boarding House and put you to bed." Sam took her arm.

Jesse Turner took Sam's arm and held it tightly. "Now, hold on, Sam. She was jest enjoyin' herself. Ain't nobody goin' to put her to bed unless hit's me."

"I'm going to put you somewhere if you don't back off, Jesse."

"Dat crowd at the Big Ball don't excite her none. She sed so herself."

"Dash right, Sam. We were just going back to the common to dance another reel," said Jenny.

"You can't dance. You can't even walk," said Sam as he pulled Jenny away with one hand and pushed Jesse away with the other.

Jesse fell against the rail fence and was about to come after Sam when Harry Bedlow came from the barn.

"Having trouble, Sam?" Harry looked at Jesse as he spoke.

"Nothing that I can't handle, Harry. I would appreciate it though if you'd see that Jesse don't bother me. I've got to get Jenny to Mrs. Eelbeck's."

"Don't you worry yourself none about Jesse. If he bothers you anymore, I'll make him give me that suit he's wearing before the night is gone."

"Ain't no harm done, Harry. Jest having a little fun—dash all," said Jesse, almost as if he were apologizing.

Sam put his left arm around Jenny's waist and took her right arm and put it around his neck. He helped her down the lane and then moved along King Street toward the Boarding House.

After they had passed the town common, Jenny looked up at Sam.

"Sam, do you really think I look like your wife, Josie? Ish that why you want to put me to bed?"

"You look more like her than anyone I've ever seen—and that's not the reason I want to put you to bed. You need rest and sleep."

"I hear your wife died in bed and now rests in the cemetery."

"Yes, Jenny."

"You don't approve of me, do you, Sam?"

"Not the way you've acted tonight. No, I don't."

"Well, I'm Jenny Hamilton, and Jenny does what she wants to do."

"I know that. I certainly know that."

"I came here to have a good time, and I wash having a good time until you put a stop to it."

"Did you ever consider what other people will say about you?"

"Who cares? I did what I wanted to do. Nobody tells Jenny Hamilton what she can or what she can't do."

With these words, Jenny's legs gave way and Sam caught her and lifted her in his arms. They were about one-half-block from the boarding house and Sam did not have very far to carry her. As he walked along with her in his arms, he thought about the first time he had seen her on the stairs at McCullen's home. He had wondered then how it would be to hold her in his arms. Now he was holding her close, and it nothing like what he had imagined.

Sam left Jenny at Mrs. Eelbeck's with a maid and hurried back to Martin's Tavern. He told Benjamin McCullen about all that had happened and learned that Archibald Hamilton had already left the ball. It was agreed that Benjamin would drive to town the next day to get Jenny. McCullen also said he was not aware that Jenny would be a problem when he asked Sam to escort her to the ball. He did, however, learn that she was more than difficult only the day before the ball, but did not anticipate any kind of misbehavior. Archibald Hamilton had talked at great length about the many problems he was having with Jenny only the day before, and was concerned that she had been staying too much with his brandy. Hamilton seemed to think that the trip to Boston would bring about a change in her behavior and habit. He had talked about consulting a physician about Jenny's problem when they got to Boston. McCullen observed that Archibald was suffering from the same problem. It seemed that both father and daughter were helpless to help each other.

Sam walked as far as the front door with the McCullens, and then spoke quietly with Mrs. Eelbeck about Jenny Hamilton. Jessica and Tom Fargo were dancing so it was most convenient for Sam to tell Mrs. Eelbeck all she wanted to know.

On his way to his room at Dudley's Tavern, Sam thought of the many imponderables that shape the lives of people and was more convinced than ever that no one would ever take Josie's place. As for Jenny Hamilton, perhaps she would find a place for herself with someone who would be generous and kind. Her beauty and station in life would attract some eager young gentleman. One thing was certain and that fact would remain unchanged—that someone would be someone else.

Chapter 9

It was as if a wisp of wind had entered an open window on a hot summer day to stir the musty air and displace it with a welcomed freshness. So it was with Sam Pickett for a brief moment in time. Upon their initial meeting, Jenny had brought to life old lingerings. She had stirred deep emotions and old feelings that he thought would once again give directions to his uncertain existence. But in the days following the ball, it was apparent that she was quite different from all he had anticipated at that first meeting. Jenny had within her being all that was repulsive to Sam. She was arrogant and even insulting at times to those who cared for her. She blamed her father for all her shortcomings and seemed to feel that he depended on her for his every comfort.

Jenny stayed at the McCullen's for a week following the ball, and Sam had on two separate visits learned much about Archibald Hamilton and Jenny Hamilton. Even though he was still overwhelmed and enthralled by her beauty, he was quick to realize that she only resembled Josie in that special way. On the day of his last visit, Sam had the opportunity to talk at great length with Jenny about all she considered meaningful in a relationship. Her most important concern in life was to be free of her father's dependence, and it seemed that she was willing to consider almost any alternative to her present situation.

"You know, father has his problems. At first I could tolerate his drinking, and with time I tried to find some way to deal with it. Finally I joined him in his effort to escape, and soon found that I, too, had come to depend on the bottle. We never drank during the day—but at night it became a regular pastime," explained Jenny as she and Sam strolled about the flower garden behind the McCullen's home.

"It's an expensive habit," warned Sam, wryly wanting to say much more.

"I'm afraid I have acquired an expensive taste, but I am sure I'll find someone to take care of the expenses."

"Now, I'm not one to offer any advice, but there are other values that you should consider that are more important when you think about what life is all about."

"Sam, you know that what matters to men is quite different. I don't think I'm so different from any other woman. I want nice things. A house with servants—and I shall require my own carriage and driver. I shall not be tied down to anyone. I'll go when I choose and stay as long as I please. These things are quite necessary. I've grown accustomed to a certain style of life. When I marry, this will certainly be understood before any ceremony takes place."

Sam held her arm as they walked along the path back to the house. "All you have mentioned about life are those possessions that will make you happy."

"You tell me, Sam. What would make you happy?"

"There are other values I think should, at least, be considered."

"Like what?" Jenny seemed interested.

"Well, like devotion, —like caring—even understanding and—most of all love."

"Those things always come with a marriage—if not with the marriage—then—later on in life."

"Josie and I shared those feelings long before we were united in marriage."

"You still haven't gotten over her, have you?"

"I suppose I never will."

"Why do you keep holding on to the past?"

"I just can't seem to let go."

"You two had something special. You may be better satisfied to hold on to those precious times that you shared with Josie. Finding someone else to share your life may be unfair to that someone, whoever she may be."

"I think you're right. I've certainly thought about that."

"Suppose through some miracle you learned that Josie had survived the smallpox and was still alive. What would you do then?"

"I'd be at her side." Sam was definite about that response.

"Josie's presence with you is still a threat to anyone who might find you attractive."

"Why do you say that?"

"Just to show you how pre-occupied you are with her. No girl in her right mind would dare try to compete with that memory."

"Oh, I see what you mean."

"Who knows, you may just have the good fortune to find someone who'll bring you more happiness than you've ever known."

"I don't think that is possible."

"Who knows? Time has a way of playing tricks with people's lives. I'm a perfect example of that."

Sam sensed that Jenny wanted to tell him more than was actually communicated. Whatever she hinted about fell short of any real meaning. Perhaps Jenny wanted to assure him that she was ready to change her life style. She did seem to want to be more like Josie.

Sam learned later that day that Jenny's trip to Boston was to deal with her father's problem and had been informed by Archibald that the purpose of the journey to Boston was to seek help for Jenny. Sam was at a loss to understand who was taking whom.

In the weeks following Jenny's departure, Sam thought about the brief relationship he had shared with the beautiful girl. She had touched his life in a very special way. Even though she was shallow, self-centered with weaknesses and unsolved problems, she was in appearance so like Josie.

In his reflections came the full realization that it would take more than appearance to satisfy his longings for someone to share his future. He was reminded of Mrs. Eelbeck's advice. "NO ONE WANTS TO TAKE JOSIE'S PLACE WITH YOU." When he thought of all the different values he considered important in a lasting relationship, his thoughts turned to Jessica. She seemed to know what she wanted and was always concerned about what he considered

Strange Wind from the Roanoke

important. There was an interest, a concern, a way of caring about others—these were the traits that he had dearly loved in Josie.

In Jenny's world there was no place for such things as a glorious sunrise or even the welcomed freshness of a shower on a hot summer day. There would be no time for the sweet smell of spring and the rebirth of life—no time for the happy laughter of children and all that comes with the union of two lovers.

But Jessica was different. She relished the coming of each new day and gloried in each sunset. It seemed that time was precious because she thought of it that way. Possessions did not matter so much to Sam or Jessica. Although things were needed and wanted, material things did not change their point of view—for what they valued was what made life full and rich. What they valued could not be owned. Nature, beauty, truth and love were a natural part of their existence and could be appreciated because they were shared.

When considering the character of the two ladies, Jessica emerged the overwhelming choice. She was a lady who could make any man proud.

To Sam's great astonishment, he soon became aware that Jessica and Tom Fargo were making plans for the future. There was talk that Jessica would be leaving Halifax for New Bern and was now trying to find a buyer for her shop. Sam listened attentively to all the rumors, and on several occasions considered going to Jessica's shop to find out for himself. Then, he thought he would be interfering with Jessica's plans. So, he dismissed the thought.

In the early days of November 1788, Sam became astounded when he learned that Jessica had closed her shop and journeyed to New Bern with Tom Fargo. He went immediately to Mrs. Eelbeck's Boarding House to get all the details.

It was late afternoon and Mrs. Eelbeck was in the kitchen preparing the supper meal for her boarders. Sam let himself in the front door, took off his coat and hat, and went immediately to the back part of the house. Mrs. Eelbeck offered Sam a chair at the small kitchen table and continued her work after she handed Sam a cup of hot tea.

"Mrs. Eelbeck, I've heard so many different rumors about Jessica, I don't know what to believe," began Sam as he stirred his tea.

"She's left, Sam. Yesterday on the noon stage. Gone to New Bern." Mrs. Eelbeck had a long oval-shaped wooden bowl in which she was kneading a large ball of dough.

"Is she planning to stay?"

"I don't know—she didn't say. I do know she will if Tom Fargo's got anything to say about it. He wants her to meet his family."

"Do they plan to marry?"

"Well, now there's been some talk about a Christmas wedding. Nothing definite, mind you."

"A Christmas wedding. That's only a little over a month away."

"When people are in love—time has little meaning."

"Do you think she'll be happy with him?"

"Why Sam Pickett—that's mighty considerate of you to be so concerned about her happiness."

"You know that I care for her. You've known all along."

"It takes more than just caring, Sam. It takes showing you care."

"It takes time, too. I don't think they've had enough time to be sure of their feelings for each other."

"With some people it does not take as much time as with others, Sam. You've certainly taken your own good time to realize how much you care about her."

"I just think one has to be sure."

"Now what makes you sure that Jessica is not sure about Tom Fargo?"

"Well, the way she talked. The way she acted when she was with me. She certainly wasn't pretending that she cared for me. I know that."

"Maybe she changed her mind about you. You were the one who moved out, remember?" Mrs. Eelbeck made the dough into biscuits, patting the dough as she placed the flattened balls on the metal tray.

"I just want what is best for her."

Mrs. Eelbeck slid the long tray into the oven, wiped her hands on her apron, and poured a cup of tea for herself. She pulled a chair back and sat at the table.

"Now Sam, you know I've always wished you two well. What is it you want me to do?"

Strange Wind from the Roanoke

"I don't know if there's anything either of us can do, now. Maybe, if you'd mention that I came by when you write her."

"She'll be back later this month. She plans to return to settle all her business here—now I do know that much."

"Perhaps I'll have a chance to speak with her then. Just when I find someone who can make me forget my past—someone else comes along."

"How about the beautiful Miss Jenny Hamilton? She looked to be the kind who could make you forget."

"She only reminded me of my past."

"She was the 'belle of the ball'. She certainly attracted all the men at the Liberty Ball."

"She'll find someone. There's no doubt. I think she'll settle for anyone who'll let her have her way."

"It's a real shame that a girl like Jenny has so little to look forward to. From all I understand, she's had a hard time since her mother's death."

"She's made it hard on herself. You know, she' not so different from me. I really haven't been very concerned about my own future—not until just recently."

"I think you've come to realize a great deal about yourself these past few months. I just hope you haven't taken too much time."

Sam looked at her quizzically and got up from the table.

"I'm not going to bother you anymore with my personal problems. There is one other thing I want to ask you. I want to move back here. I feel more comfortable here than any other place in Halifax. Have you rented Jessica's room?"

"No, you can move in any time you've a mind to. I'll hold it for you. There are some personal things of hers still up there. She stored all she left in her trunks. I thought I'd just leave her stuff in her room until she comes for it."

"I'll be by later with my clothes. I'll spend the night here," said Sam, as he walked away from the table.

Mrs. Eelbeck turned to the stove and peeked in. She looked up and said, "Sam, Oney is out back making soap. She wants to talk to you before you go back to the office. I'm glad you came by."

Sam was putting his coat on as he walked past Mrs. Eelbeck. "I'm glad, too. I'll see you later. I'll just go out the backdoor."

103

Oney was making soap in a large iron pot. Sam could see that she had already made one pot and was starting to prepare lye for another. Oney nodded as Sam came near.

"We saves all the wood ashes from the fireplace then we put them in a barrel. We pours in the water and let it soak in the ashes and trickle out a hole at the bottom of the barrel." Sam leaned over to get a closer look. "That is what we call 'lye'. Now, don't you touch that. When the lye is ready, we take it to the kettle and boils it into the grease and fats that we've saved up over the past several months. Then we cooks it slowly 'til it thickens and forms a soft yellow soap. I puts some special scents to make the lye more tolerable."

"Mrs. Eelbeck said you wanted to talk to me," said Sam, changing the subject.

Well, Mr. Dudley told me that you wanted to talk to me."

"Oh, I have wanted to ask you about a dream that I keep having. I just can't get rid of it. Dudley said you might be of some help."

"Tell me about it while Ah'm about my work," suggested Oney.

Sam told her each detail about the dream that had been so much a part of his sadness. When he had finished, Oney promised that she would do what she could to find some meaning to the nightmare.

"You know, Mrs. Eelbeck is lucky to have you to help her."

"She is not as lucky as I am to have her. She is somebody special and the love she gives to all her friends jists comes back to her. Love is one thang dat we can give away and never miss it." Oney made a little rhyme. She said: "LOVE COMES TO US IN A SPECIAL WAY. THE BEST WAY TO GET IT IS TO GIVE IT AWAY."

Sam had never thought of love with that particular meaning. He felt a sudden insight that he had not expected and it would make him look at life in a different way. He wondered if other people had similar experiences. Perhaps these moments come to all who consider such things.

He felt that he would leave Oney's presence somewhat changed and he was feeling good because he felt that change would be for the better. Somehow Sam felt relieved that he had told Oney about his dream. He walked quickly to Dudley's Tavern to gather his belongings and told Dudley of his decision to move back to Mrs.

Strange Wind from the Roanoke

Eelbeck's. "I don't blame you, Sam," said Dudley. "I just might do the same thing one of these days."

Sam was one of the few people in Halifax who would understand the hidden meaning of Dudley's statement.

It was dark by the time Sam took his valise and clothes up to Jessica's room. He took a candle from the hall table and was soon lighting other candles in the room. He threw his valise on the bed, opened it and put his clothes in the highboy. As he moved about the room, he sensed a feminine odor that was a part of Jessica's presence. The familiar odor touched off impressions from the past—he remembered the day of the picnic—the night of the LIBERTY BALL—all those special glances and gestures that had been a part of their close relationship. Being in the room where she had spent so many hours—inhaling the intoxicating aroma of her perfume—using the same bed where she had slept, made it seem as if she were close enough to touch. Sam sat down on the bed beside the valise. Now the realization that Jessica was beyond his reach slowly began to dawn on him. In his quandary he looked about the room as if he were searching for the answers on the walls and ceiling.

He reached again into the valise to finish the unpacking and his hand touched Josie's leather-bound journal. He held it tenderly in his hand and thought of the many times in his past when he had turned the pages and how he had found comfort in the reading of her endearing words.

Sam got up and put the valise at the end of the bed and then returned to make himself comfortable. He lay on his left side so the light from the candle would serve him better. The cover of the journal was in Josie's flourishing script. THE JOURNAL OF JOSIE HAMILTON.

At the beginning was an account of the Hamilton's preparation to leave Halifax back on April 12, 1776. At the end of the entry was a poem. Sam imagined that he could hear the voice of Josie and the words came as a whisper from her lips.

> Sam does not know it
> And I've been afraid to show it
> But this feeling deep inside
> Can find no place to hide
> Now, I must let him know

I'll never let him go
I'll stand by him when times are bad
I'll cheer him up when he is sad
That's how I'll let him know
I'll never let him go.
Together we'll face all that is to be
And he'll find love and trust in me
Then I'm sure he'll know
I'll never let him go
When our years are past away
And we both are old and gray
I'll still let him know
I'll never let him go
I'll never let him go

Sam smiled at the written thoughts of Josie. He thumbed through the pages to read from certain passages that were dear to him. He paused on October 1, 1778 entry to read about George's enlistment in the British Army. While staying in New Bern, John Hamilton too had accepted his commission as Colonel in the service of the king. The account told of Josie's deep concern for her family and herself. Sam read aloud a special poem. This time in Josie's life was hard and her words told of her uncertain future.

What is my life all about?
Wonder when I'll find out
Why my dreams of yesterday
All have fallen by the way
There was a time when love was mine
And I was happy then
Where did it go, when will I know
Just where my love has been
What is my life all about?
Wonder when I'll find out
My thoughts have been about him
Since I've been without him
And I wonder if he
Will ever come back to me
What is my life all about?

Strange Wind from the Roanoke

> Wonder when I'll find out
> Maybe the future will bring
> A song we both can sing
> Then I'll have no doubt
> What my life is all about?
> What is my life all about?
> Wonder when I'll find out

Sam slowly turned through the pages stopping to read the entry about George's death at Guilford Court House. Josie had titled this poem—I'll ALWAYS REMEMBER HIM

> I'll always remember him
> I'll always remember him
> Those who have met him
> May soon forget him
> But I shall remember him
> He was kind to me
> Good and kind to me
> This boy in my life
> Brought joy to my life
> And I shall remember him
> We played on the village green
> And roamed the hills and streams
> We were together, always together
> Sharing each other's dreams
> I'll always remember him
> I'll always remember him
> Those who have met him
> May soon forget him
> But I shall remember him
> Now he's gone from me
> But there will always be
> A place for my friend
> Where love will never end
> For I shall remember him.

After reading the account of her mother's death, Sam turned to the final entry. The last page was written in 1781 while Josie and he were living in Edenton. Sam's lips moved but no audible sound came from his lips.

> The time has come for me to leave you
> It's hard for me to have to go
> There's so much I want to tell you
> There's so much you need to know
> Soon, there will be another
> Who'll want to hold you near
> And she'll say all the right words
> That you long to hear
> Just remember that I love you
> And if you don't know what to say
> Tell her life is for the living
> And I'm sure you'll find a way
> Love can be wonderful
> Life can be sublime
> If the one you love
> Will love you all the time
> There's much more I want to tell you
> That in time you'll come to know
> Just let me say how much I love you
> One more time before I go
> Oh, my dear—I love you so.

Sam closed the journal and lay back on the bed. He looked about the room at the distorted shapes seen through tearful eyes. There was such devotion that Sam almost felt guilty that he ever seriously considered any kind of relationship with Jessica Jackson. What stirred him more than any other entry was the final one. Josie penned it while she was on her deathbed.

Wiping the tears from his eyes with the sleeve of his shirt, Sam bounded to the floor and placed the journal in the valise and closed it. Thoughts of Josie and the compassion captured in her words occupied his mind as he prepared for bed.

When the candles were extinguished, he lay back on the bed and thought. Sleep came slowly and Sam tossed and turned in his restive slumber—his mind darting—here and there to recall special times from his past. The pieces began to take shape and form and even began to fit into a pattern that made sense. It was after midnight before Sam came to fully understand that Josie would remain forever in his thoughts. No one could fill the void left by her. He felt satisfied that he had made the right decision about Jessica. She deserved happiness. He knew she would find her place. He also knew that his life would always be shadowed by the relationship he had shared with his beloved Josie. The very memory of her was more important to him than any relationship he could find with any other companion.

Chapter 10

Since the Anti-Federalists under the capable leadership of Willie Jones had refused to adopt the Constitution, enough strength had been mustered by the Federalists to get a second ratifying convention. It was quickly decided that the third Monday in November of 1789 would be set aside for that purpose.

When Davie returned to Halifax, he put forth an effort to get all the debates that had ensued at Fayetteville into print. These printed circulars were distributed to leaders throughout the state. Articles were written, speeches were given, and newspapers headlined the issues that divided the people—the question of adoption was before the people.

Sam had never seen Davie so consumed by anything. The harder Davie worked for ratification, the greater the demands at the office, and consequently, Sam could not recall when so much work had to be done in such a short period of time. Correspondence with James Iredell demanded much of Davie's time for these two were now laying plans to inform the people and to influence those who voted not to ratify the Constitution.

The mood of the people seemed to be changing. There was a report that certain Anti-Federalists had been hung in effigy at Tarboro

Strange Wind from the Roanoke

and the Federalists were strong for another convention. Pamphlets were circulated that strongly criticized the Anti-Federalists.

Momentum now seemed to be with the Federalists as new developments sided their cause. The new government was operating without North Carolina's ratification, and it seemed to be working most effectively. Times were getting better and the people were becoming more prosperous as prices increased and trade flourished. There was now an important movement by James Madison who had proposed the new amendments with the Bill of Rights. Davie was so elated about Madison's move that he wrote him a personal letter to express his deep gratitude. In Davie's letter, he was careful to point out that the amendments contained in the Bill of Rights were not all the Anti-Federalists of North Carolina had requested. Even though the amendment contained in Bill of Rights represented the strong convictions of the Anti-Federalists in North Carolina, it by no means answered all the objections the party had about the new Constitution.

There was a chill in the early morning air as Sam walked from Dudley's Tavern. He picked up his mail and was now on his way to the office. He had decided earlier to do some surveying at the backside of the cemetery for the Reverend Ford; therefore he had dressed in his old work clothes.

He had been at Mrs. Eelbeck's for two weeks and was happy with his decision to move back. The journal that Josie left behind cleared his mind of so many uncertainties. He had been reminded of her sincere devotion. His thoughts now returned to the words that Josie had written. She had such appreciation of the time they had shared—such—understanding—such compassion. When he thought over those experiences they had shared,— new insights,— new appreciations,— new impressions began to play on his mind. The many expressions she had written in her journal would sustain him for the rest of his life.

Sam turned off Market Street and felt a gusty wind coming from the Roanoke, so he hurried along. After he had a brisk fire going in the small fireplace, he took off his heavy coat and sorted the mail. There were several letters to Davie and a newspaper only six days old, which was published in New Bern. Sam placed the letters on Davie's large desk, then moved Davie's chair to the window to catch the morning light. He unfolded the newspaper and settled down in the large chair. The headline was a disturbing account of the struggle that was raging in France. The French were fighting for their freedom, but it all seemed rather complicated to Sam. Yet, there were accounts similar to the great Revolution that had taken place in America. From what he could understand, the French National Assembly had adopted the Declaration of the Rights of Man back in August of 1789 and made it the preamble to their Constitution. The name Marquis de Lafayette was the only name Sam recognized. It seemed that Lafayette was involved in the operation of the new government.

Sam became fascinated with all he read. The first Article of the French Constitution stated that "men are born and remain free and equal in their rights", and Article II defended such rights as liberty, property, security and the right to resist oppression. There were other Articles that guaranteed all the aforementioned rights. Liberty was defined as the "power to do whatever does not injure another."

Sam looked out the window and thought about Jefferson's DECLARATION OF INDEPENDENCE. Jefferson had borrowed many ideas from the Europeans and now it seemed they wanted to use some of these ideas to express the rights of the French people.

The French were now seeking aid from the United States, but there was great concern that we were not yet ready to get involved in any European problems.

Sam pushed the chair back behind Davie's desk and put the newspaper aside. He reached for his coat and black cocked hat, and then opened the door to the small storage room. After gathering his surveying gear and shovel, he left the office.

He spent the next two hours at the backside of the cemetery and used his shovel to trench around the three new plots that were large enough for four graves each. As he walked back among the stones, he could see there had been much erosion from the heavy rains that had come in the fall of 1789. Now, wanting to check on Josie's grave, he walked to that special mound. There was a small gully at the base of her grave, so Sam put down his pack and scooped several shovel loads of fresh earth and filled in the part that had been washed away. He then turned to Sadie Jackson's grave and spent some time there. The same trench that had eroded Josie's grave continued across Sadie's grave.

It was after noon when Sam finished his work. He picked up his pack and shovel and walked again to the base of Josie's grave. He stood there for a moment with his back toward King Street. He put his

Strange Wind from the Roanoke

gear down and took Josie's letter from his coat. He read it reverently and silently to himself. Sam felt almost as if he were communicating with Josie as he read. Although he had read the letter many times, there was a feeling that the words now held greater significance than ever. It was almost as if she were speaking to him from the grave. This strange sensation caused him to fold the letter quickly and insert it once more into the worn envelope. He held it tightly in his right hand.

"Thank you, Sam," came a soft voice from behind him.

Sam turned quickly and was surprised to see Jessica looking at the work he had done at Sadie Jackson's grave.

"Jessica! Jessica! You scared the life outa me! What are you doing here?"

"Mrs. Eelbeck sent me to find you."

Sam looked at Jessica standing before him. She was wearing a deep green walking dress. Her jacket had a tight-fitting bodice. A brisk wind was blowing her skirt and the long pale green kerchief that hung loosely about her shoulders.

The wind caught and tugged at her green wide-brimmed hat, but a long black ribbon tied securely beneath her chin kept it from blowing away. Her blonde curls danced to the tempo of the blowing gust of wind.

Suddenly a strange and chilling wind swept from the Roanoke and was swirling about them as if it were intended for them alone. Sam looked at Jessica. The wind was cyclonic and settled at the very spot where they stood.

There was a tug at the envelope, which contained Josie's last letter. The letter flew from Sam's right hand up into the twisting wind. Sam tried desperately to grasp it but it was hopeless.

"Sam what is it?"

"The letter, it just seemed to be taken from me by the wind," said Sam. There was a tremble in his voice.

"What kind of letter?"

"I had Josie's last letter in my hand and it's gone."

They both looked at the swirling cloud of dust as the mass moved upward and away from them.

Sam turned to Jessica. "What just happened was not a natural act of the elements."

"Why do you say that, Sam?"

"It just doesn't seem possible," he said, shaking his head. "I was holding the letter too tight."

"Do you suppose it just may mean something, Sam? You know, you had to let go, don't you?"

"But it wasn't of my own doing."

"Perhaps it wasn't. Strange things do sometimes happen to us that are not of our own doing."

"I sensed a presence—even before you came."

"There will always be a presence in this spot for you and me, Sam."

"The wind died down and Sam looked into Jessica's eyes. "Are you back in Halifax to stay?'

"I never intended to stay in New Bern. I knew that even before I left. There's too much to hold me here. I would be as an alien anywhere else. I, like you, cannot separate the present from the past. I think it's good to belong. Everybody should feel the need of a special place or a special person. Tom will be moving to Halifax. We intend to make our home here.

Sam was somewhat disturbed by what he was hearing. "You mean you and Tom Fargo intend to be married?"

"Sam, you know, as well as I do, that no one could ever take the place of Josie. I didn't come here to tell you of my affairs. Mrs. Eelbeck sent me to fetch you. That Hamilton girl is at the McCullen Plantation waiting to see you."

"Jenny Hamilton back in Halifax? I wonder why she wants to see me." Sam picked up his plumb line and gear.

"I have my own ideas about that, but I'd rather not say what they are, Sam,"said Jessica, now walking briskly beside Sam.

"I'm happy for you, Jessica. I know you'll find your place here with Tom."

"He is most kind to me, Sam. I'm sure we both share the same affection. It has to be both ways, you know."

Sam smiled with a knowing look that told her he understood. Somehow the union of Jessica and Tom Fargo made sense and he was surprised how well he was feeling about the forthcoming marriage. Deep down, he realized that Jessica would always remain a close friend but nothing more could ever come from his relationship with her.

Strange Wind from the Roanoke

When they reached King Street, Sam said goodbye to Jessica and started toward the office to store his gear.

Turning up the walkway, Sam looked once again to the spot where he and Jessica had stood in the cemetery. The wind was providential—prophetic—how else could he think of all that had just happened other than a force from beyond had communicated to his very soul.

As he started up the walk to the office he saw Looney Oney coming up the road from the Roanoke River. As she came closer, Sam wondered what powers the psychic woman had been employing at the river.

She was coming from the same direction the wind came from thought Sam, closely watching the approaching figure.

"WIND THAT'S STRANGE—WILL BRING CHANGE," now echoed in Sam's mind.

Oney came closer. Sam sat on the bench and waited for Oney to come his way.

"Where've you been, Oney?"

"Ah wah down to the river, but Ah can't do no good de way de wind's been playing tricks wid de water. Ah wah fishing from Mr. Willie's dock when this here twisting wind came churning through the water. Messed up mah fishing—scared what few fish there wah halfway to the coast." Oney looked to the distant clouds as she spoke. She sat down on the bench.

"Did the wind come down the river?"

"Hit moved at the speed of a sloop—no faster than a boat," said Oney.

"Where did it go when it left the river?" questioned Sam.

"Hit moved straight to Willie Jones' dock and after a spell hit moved up de hill toward de river road. About halfway up de hill it just stopped and stayed. Strangest wind Ah ever saw. Just stopped and stayed. Then, after a spell hit moved along the river road toward King Street."

Sam looked closely at Oney. "We brought Josie to Willie Jones' dock.—and the hill—that's where the horse slipped and fell lame—when we were taking Josie's body to the cemetery."

"What hoss?" Oney was trying to understand.

"When the carriage with Josie's body started up the hill, the horse slipped and fell lame. Allen Jones hitched his own horse to the

Maxville Burt Williams

carriage and led the lame horse —just behind the funeral procession —to the livery stable," Sam could see that Oney was understanding, because she just kept shaking her head up and down.

"So—dat explains it. Couldn't understand —makes sense now." Oney seemed satisfied.

"What makes sense, Oney? Do you think it was Josie's spirit? That wind came to the spot I stood and took the last letter that Josie had written right outa my hand."

"Oney don't explain nothing she don't know. Oney sees strange thangs—but Oney don't make them come to pass." Oney shook her head as she spoke.

"What did you make of the dream that I told you about. Did you ever have time to think about it?"

"I thought about that dream. In passing Ah stopped at the grave of Miss Josie and stood over her resting-place. Now, Ah made the visit three times and nothing happened. After three times, it ain't no used to go back. Ah just had the feeling that Ah was talking to the dirt."

"Well, I'm grateful for any kind of explanation. I want to thank you for telling me what you saw, Oney."

Oney seemed to be weary from all that had happened to her at the Roanoke River.

"The spirits have been too much wid me today. Ah jest don't know how Ah'll be able to see any peace. Ah don't git no sleep at tall when the spirits are about me." Oney looked toward the cemetery as if she were talking about the dead.

"What can I do to help, Oney?" Sam seemed sympathetic.

"About the onliest way to calm dem and put dem to rest is fer me to take up wid another spirit. Ah've found that the spirit in a good wine'll keep all the other spirits in their proper place. Do you know how Ah could manage to come upon that kind of spirit, Mr. Pickett?"

Sam reached into his pocket and withdrew a silver piece.

"You don't change, Oney. I think I've heard that story before."

"Did you believe me, when I told it to you down by Quanky Creek?"

"Here, Oney I don't want you to be plagued with any spirit on my account. Get you a bottle and keep your spirits high." He handed the silver coin to Oney.

Strange Wind from the Roanoke

Oney's eyes lit up at the sight of the money. She grabbed it quicker than a frog could capture a fly. "You can count on me doing just dat, Mr. Pickett. Me and the spirits will be in good accord tonight. Ah feel lack Ah need to give you something for all your good deeds. So Ah'll give you something to take with you to the grave. Remember what Ah'm telling you, now. This is something that comes from deep inside."

Oney seemed really concerned that Sam heed her words.
"DON'T LOOK BACK ON YESTERDAY
IF IT BRANGS YOU SORROW
LOOK AT TODAY IN A DIFFERENT WAY
AND THANK ABOUT TOMORROW"

Sam looked at Oney as she smiled and waved goodbye. He was always fascinated by the very presence of Looney Oney. Sam sensed that she had wisdom beyond her own understanding. Sam thought that the epigram that Oney had expressed was something special. Now, if Benjamin Franklin had made such a statement, the whole world would know about it. Sam wondered about all the great ideas that had been wasted because the person who made the contribution was not well known.

He watched Oney as she moved along King Street. There were two little "dust devils" that seemed to follow at her heels. Sam wondered if perhaps they had been spawned by the cyclonic wind that took Josie's letter. She seemed to lean to her right and appeared to be falling but her inertia kept her to her path.

Sam picked up his shovel and gear from the bench as he watched Oney turn onto Market Street toward Dudley's Tavern. Sam smiled as he thought about the great pleasure he was able to provide Oney and how he had come to think about her much the same as Dudley. She was a special person. She had given Sam insight that would make a difference and the difference would be for a change that would be for the better. There was wisdom in the words of Oney that would apply to anyone. He decided that he would look forward to tomorrow and stop worrying about all that had happened in his past.

Sam immediately went to the office and was putting away his gear when Dudley's tavern boy came bursting into the office with a letter extended from his right hand.

"Mr. Dudley told me to fetch this letter to you. It just came in on the stage."

Sam reached into his pocket and handed the boy a farthing. The boy grinned at the sight of the money and hurried from the room. Sam smiled and looked at the letter. It was from William R. Davie. He opened it and read it silently.

Sam's eyes hurried across the lines and before he had read the entire letter, he looked up and said aloud, THE CONVENTION AT FAYETTEVILLE HAS RATIFIED THE UNITED STATES CONSITUTION by a vote of 195 to 77 on November 21, 1789. Davie also mentioned that the convention had adopted a plan for a state university. A state university was something that Davie had worked for and was now beginning to take shape and form.

He folded the letter and was soon on his way to Dudley's Tavern.

Upon entering the tavern, Sam went to the counter to tell Dudley the good news. "Davie said he wants you and me to see that all the people are at the common tomorrow at noon. He'll be back by that time. He said he wants to speak to the people."

Dudley's bulbous eyes lit up. "Sam, we've got to get busy if the word is to reach all the people by tomorrow noon."

"We'll send riders out to all the people throughout the countryside."

"The townspeople need to be told today," suggested Dudley.

"I'll tell all the people out McCullen's way tomorrow morning." Sam thought of his meeting with Jenny Hamilton.

"I'll tell everybody who comes in here to go out and tell everybody else."

"The word must be sent to all—who without knowing—now belong to a United America," shouted Sam, waving goodbye to Dudley.

Chapter 11

Sam sent young boys scurrying through the streets yelling and telling people to tell other people about the meeting on the common. All who lived along the streets that ran perpendicular to King Street would be told. People in all the shops, all the taverns, all the inns and all the businesses were to be informed.

It was late afternoon when Sam returned to the tavern. He and Dudley talked at great length about the next day's activities. They both agreed that all the people in town and most of the people in the surrounding countryside would be told. Sam felt a real satisfaction just knowing that by noon the next day there would be a great gathering at the common to welcome Davie and the other delegates back to Halifax.

It was twilight as Sam walked to Mrs. Eelbeck's Boarding House. When he entered, Mrs. Eelbeck was clearing away the table.

"Where've you been, Sam?"

"I've been all over town telling the people the good news about what happened in Fayetteville."

"I heard the news and it's about time. Did Jessica tell you that the Hamilton girl is waiting for you at McCullens?"

"Yes, I was working at the cemetery. I didn't think there was any reason to leave all I had to do."

"Well, sit down and I'll get you a bowl of stew. It's about all that's left."

When Sam had finished his meal, he excused himself and went to his room. He was tired but only good thoughts occupied his mind. He placed a candle near his bed and reached for the almanac on the table. Mrs. Eelbeck knew that he liked to keep informed and reading the almanac was always something special. He read some select passages from the book and noticed that there was a prediction of snow for the next day.

He was restive and sleep came slowly. He dreamed of a wedding, but his bride had a veil that hid her identity. Life seemed to be filled with enthusiasm—there was eagerness—a longing—to be all things to all people. He had an appetite great enough to devour each coming day—life was real to him in his dreams. In his dream, he dreamed that he had climbed to the top of a mountain and touched the clouds of time and he could see eternity. It was so real to him that he felt his dream was an omen of what was to come. He hoped that the dream would in some way help him cope with the future.

Upon awakening, Sam sat up in bed, but he did not get up. He lay back with is hands locked behind his head and contemplated the meaning of his dream. He was still light-headed, fresh and alert. No semblance of anything disturbing entered his mind. He felt a burden had been lifted from his shoulders. Perhaps it had been lifted from him by the swirling wind that had touched him in the cemetery. One thing was certain—he had not dreamed of Josie's funeral—which—in itself—was unusual. He hoped with all his soul that his dream was a hint of things to come. Although he had slept later than he had intended, he was up and dressed by the time Dudley came to the Boarding House for the eight o'clock breakfast. After quickly gulping some side-meat, biscuits, grits, and coffee, he hurried to Harry Bedlow's shop to ask that a flat wagon be taken to the corner of Market and King Street to be used as a platform. Davie needed something to raise him above the crowd. Bedlow assured Sam that all would be ready by noon. Bedlow also mentioned that his wife had returned from Edenton and he had promised he would put away the bottle if she would stay with him.

From the blacksmith shop, Sam walked across King Street to Martin's Livery and hitched Davie's horse to a gig. Soon he was on his way to the McCullens.

Strange Wind from the Roanoke

As he rode along the road, he thought how Davie had risen above the adversities that had plagued the state. Now there was to be a joining of North Carolina to the Union. Much of the victory in North Carolina could be traced to the great effort put forth by Davie who had worked untiringly for this glorious day. His character and his statesmanship were influences that now shaped the mood and thinking of the people.

UNION—the word seemed to have strength in it. Now North Carolina, too, belonged—there was a deep sense of security—a feeling of hope for the future— for North Carolina was at last a part of the great United States.

Sam thought of the union of North Carolina with the other states as a marriage. A marriage of thirteen participants who would eventually give birth to the populace. The Constitution was like a holy contract—a license that would forever bind the states to each other so firmly that there could be no separation. The national government would be parents to guide and direct the states, which were now, mature enough to consider marriage. The mother —the legislature, would make the rules and the father— the executive, would see that they were enforced. The national court would serve as the judge who would always be present to settle any difficulties that could not otherwise be concluded.

With this neat concept Sam was aware that the family would grow to take in other members and there would be some members who would be strong and some who would be weak. It would be the responsibility of the parents to treat each member with love and respect. There would always be the people who would be entrusted with the final authority. The people would act as the soul of the nation. For without a soul there could be no guiding will to shape the character of the great family.

Sam briefly compared the new nation to several large families he knew in Halifax. With children there were always conflicts, interests, and characteristics that made the individual children different. Each child often thought only of himself and his own interest, without considering the welfare of other members of the family. With maturity many of these problems could be eliminated. Sam hoped the new nation would not have to suffer the stresses and strains he had seen in some of the families he knew.

Perhaps the painful period was now a thing of the past. He felt confident that the national government would act with enough perspicuity and wisdom to meet the future difficulties with resolute understanding. The nation was strong enough to accept any burden that was too heavy for a state to shoulder.

Sam was so possessed with his analogy that he passed two farmhouses without stopping to tell the people of the meeting at the town common.

On his way to McCullen's Plantation, he wondered just what had caused Jenny Hamilton to return to Halifax. Perhaps her visit to Boston had brought change. Stranger things had happened. Thoughts of Jenny Hamilton still occupied his mind as he tied his horse to the hitching post in front of McCullen's house.

When Sam rapped the bronze knocker, the large front door opened and Rebecca McCullen stood there with outstretched arms.

"Welcome, Sam." Rebecca McCullen looked beyond Sam. "I think I just saw a snowflake."

"It just started as I was tying my horse."

"We expected you yesterday." Rebecca held the door open for Sam.

"I'll tell you about yesterday sometime when I've got the time. Yesterday was a long day."

"Well, come on in. She's waiting for you in the guestroom. I've got work to do, so I'll leave you two alone."

Rebecca gave Sam a tender smile. Sam smiled back but did not understand the meaning of that special look. It was as if she were telling him a well kept secret that was now being revealed to him for the first time.

When Sam entered the room, he saw a young woman sitting on the red upholstered divan, which was across the room from the doorway. He stopped just as he entered and looked closely at the lady clothed in purple. A black small-brimmed felt hat covered her hair. A black silk veil hid her face. Sam moved a step closer.

"Sam—Sam Pickett," came a soft voice from behind the veil. She stood.

Something stirred deep inside of Sam. Could this be possible? Was it all a prank that could only have been contrived by Jenny Hamilton? No—no—no—it was nothing of the kind. It was real—it was really happening—for standing before him the young woman

Strange Wind from the Roanoke

slowly lifted the veil from her face to reveal several faded facial scars. Those sad telling marks that could only have come from one who suffered the dreaded smallpox.

"JOSIE—JOSIE—." Sam rushed to her and put his arms around her and held her close. If this were an apparition, he would not allow his grasp to slip. Not this time. They both sat on the sofa in an hysterical embrace. Both laughed and cried at the same time for an enchanted moment. The moment led to another moment. It was a time that was precious and would never come again.

When they had gathered their senses, Josie began.

"Father told me that you, too, likely contracted the smallpox. So many died, you know. Then, when I started writing to you, I never received any answers to my letters. I was satisfied that Father was right."

"I never got any letters, Josie."

"I know that now. Father had all the letters stopped before they were ever posted. He told me all about that before he sailed for England last week."

"Why didn't Jenny tell me that you were alive?"

"Father and Uncle Archibald corresponded frequently. I'm sure Father made certain demands when they journeyed to Boston last year. The trip to Boston was to deliver some valuables that Father had left with Uncle Archibald when he left New Bern to join the British. Father often spoke of the money he had loaned to Uncle Archibald."

"Did they tell you that I was alive?"

"When they left Boston to come back to New Bern, Uncle Archibald told Father that I should be told. Just this last month Father decided it was time for me to know."

"It's too good to be true, Josie,"

"Father asked for your forgiveness and said he hoped that my inheritance would somehow help make up for all the pain he had caused both of us. He is truly sorry. After his visit here to Halifax, I think he realized you were as devoted to me as I am to you. He told me how you helped him get free from the stocks. He said you saved his life."

"So now your father is on his way to England?"

"He asked me if I'd like to sail with him, but I would not consider it. I told father I would rather live here with Uncle

Archibald. Well, that's when he revealed everything. He truly has high regard for you, Sam. Can you ever forgive him?"

"At this moment I could forgive the devil. All those years I thought you were at rest in the cemetery."

"It cost Father twenty shillings to get the attendant at the quarantine house to put my name on that coffin of dirt when it was shipped up the Roanoke to Halifax."

"I still don't understand how you were moved without my knowing it."

"Well, when father heard how sick I was, he felt the doctors in Petersburg could give me better treatment. Father was immune to the disease, so he came and literally spirited me away. When I was well enough to travel, I went with Father to Boston where he had been given a position as Consul for the King."

"Weren't you aware of what was happening?"

"I was delirious but only part of the time. Father told the attendant he was taking me to another doctor. You know how persuasive he can be. The money he paid the attendant made it seem the right thing to do, I suppose." Josie seemed to be apologizing.

"Some people will do anything for money. I hope your father finds happiness in England."

"I doubt he'll ever return. He provided me with an inheritance that should sustain us for as long as we both shall live."

After many questions and answers, Sam realized that what John Hamilton had done for Josie was done because of his deep love and concern for his daughter. There was no hatred for his father-in-law. Allowing Josie to come to him now was enough to make up for all those wasted years.

Benjamin McCullen came to the house from the barn and told everybody that it was beginning to snow. He rigged the sleigh for Sam to use to get back to Halifax. For the next hour, there was rejoicing with Benjamin and Rebecca McCullen. Sam felt a closeness to the McCullens that came with this special time in his life. Rebecca took great pride in the role she played. Soon, Sam told Josie about the meeting at the common and how important it was for him to get back to Halifax to meet William R. Davie.

Rebecca McCullen was reluctant to allow them to leave and would only consider it if they promised to return the next day for

Strange Wind from the Roanoke

Thanksgiving dinner. She promised Sam that this would be one Thanksgiving he would long remember.

On the way to Halifax, Josie sat close to Sam on the sleigh. As they rode along the snow-covered road, Sam remembered the big snow two years ago. The great beauty and wonder that now touched everything in sight also touched him. He and Joise were both in an imaginary world—a wonderland. They talked at a hectic pace and at times both were talking at the same time and much of what was said did not make any sense.

Sam said he thought his work would be enough to provide for them. He told Josie he had once considered attending Princeton to study law. Now, that was out of the question. Office work was too confining. He liked the idea of working outside. He remembered that values in life were determined by what one thought would bring happiness. Happiness had always been an ambiguous word that was hard for Sam to define. It had a different meaning to different people. What could be better than a job that brought him pleasure while he was making a living for his family?

From the conversation emerged a plan for the future. Josie made Sam aware of the money that her father had forwarded to the Bank at New Bern. Sam thought Josie and he knew they were experiencing something rare. A second chance for happiness was something that only came to a blessed few. It had been a long time since Sam felt the comfort of knowing he could have a future that would bring him love and happiness. He was aware that his grasp for a better life was again within his reach. He made a promise to himself he would hold on to the blessing as long as he had the strength.

It was almost noon when Sam stepped down from the sleigh to tie up at Mrs. Eelbeck's Boarding House. The snow had stopped and the temperature had risen. Suddenly Sam became aware of a stately black carriage coming down King Street. He immediately knew it to be Davie's coach. Davie waved from the window and people along the street joined to form a great train as they moved toward the town common. Sam held out his arm and Josie grabbed hold as they joined the throng of people walking in the wake of the coach. Sam felt good just having Josie at his side. There was comfort in her touch—a feeling of belonging to someone. It had been a long time since he had the satisfaction of knowing the one he held close was as deeply devoted to him as he was to her.

Maxville Burt Williams

Sam urged Josie to hasten, and they, too, were soon pushing and picking their way among the thick crowd to get closer to the coach.

After much maneuvering and shoving, they stood at the edge of the large crowd. Sam could see William R. Davie, John Ashe, and Allen Jones ascend the wagon that served as the platform.

"We need to get closer. I want to hear every word," said Sam as he tugged at Josie's arm.

"We'll have to be satisfied, Sam. The crowd is too thick."

"Follow me, Josie. Just hold my hand."

They skirted the crowd and nudged their way around Davie's coach. They eased their way among unwilling people who reluctantly gave way to them. Sam was not satisfied until they were standing directly in front of the platform.

Sam and Josie looked at the three delegates who were waving to the great gathering. From the crowd came a deafening roar and Davie did not seem to be in any hurry to quieten them. He appeared to be enjoying the great wave of enthusiasm coming from the excitement that stirred the emotions of all he looked upon.

When the great welcome had died down, Davie stepped forward as Ashe and Jones took a chair just to each side of Davie.

"My friends—my good friends—we have been for many years in need of the news that has preceded our coming. I know that many of you have heard the good news—however, I must make you aware of what this nation now requires of you.

We must never lose sight of our freedom—our right to be ourselves—our freedom of conscience. What we have done in Fayetteville is to guarantee the right that all people will be protected as they seek to live among their neighbors. Unless we have strength in the law and a national government to insure freedom to all—then — there can be no liberty for anyone. We must now give our loyalty to our country and trust those in office to serve us in our best interests. The rule of the people is the foundation of this new nation. When our government fails to recognize this basic relationship—then the time will again be ripe for change.

We have instituted within our system certain guarantees that no branch of government shall ever become so powerful as to rule without control. Now, we are a part of this great system. North Carolina is in harmony and at peace with the times. We shall look

Strange Wind from the Roanoke

toward our leaders for guidance and wisdom—wisdom to know that we are different. If we were the same, then there would have been no need for the Revolution. We are all different in our destinies, and our new Constitution will give us the right to be what we are—and while we are different, we shall always have to guard the precious right to be different. If we ever become so much the same, then the time will again come for brave men to stand strong in the right to be different. This new Constitution shall always give support to those who dare to contest the idea that we must always be as all others. We have fought and won our freedom—now we must learn to live with restraint. We must understand that our freedom is not complete freedom and can be defined as meaningful only when it is used with wisdom and compassion for our fellowman. We all know that there are many problems that we must overcome. Slavery is an institution that countries in Europe are abolishing and with time we, too, must consider what will be the remedy for our own country. We can only hope that time will be kind, and we shall get to where we are destined without too much hardship.

All people shall be equally treated and all people shall have rights and freedom—and because of these rights and freedoms, they shall be what destiny has decreed for them and not what men, who rule arbitrarily, shall determine.

Be always mindful that we shall be equal—one to the other in the eyes of the law. Thus, there shall come security for each of us to grow to our fullest potential. Our new plan of government now gives us the freedom to seek our own destinies and at the same time it will protect us while we are about our endeavors. God bless all of you, and I sincerely thank all of you for this great welcome."

There was a tumultuous swell of applause followed by shouting and loud talk that continued for several minutes.

Sam looked at Josie. She smiled and Sam took her in his arms. There was more to the embrace than he had expected. She held him tightly and Sam felt a great security—a need to be needed. In the midst of the cheering crowd, Sam returned the embrace with warm enthusiasm. In many ways he felt the time was as much his as it was William R. Davie. Now he, too, was in harmony with the scheme of things.

"We are now a part of something great, Josie," said Sam.

"I shall always be at your side, Sam."

Maxville Burt Williams

"And I'll never let you go."

Sam looked into Josie's clear blue eyes and saw his future dancing there. He knew —there was no doubt— he was once again fortunate to be among those who were called BLEST.

THE END

ABOUT THE AUTHOR

Maxville Burt Williams was born in Sharpsburg, North Carolina and now resides in Enfield, North Carolina. He graduated from Enfield High School and attended East Carolina University. While at the university, he became interested in writing and had one play produced by the East Carolina Playhouse and another published by the University. After graduating from East Carolina University with a degree in History and a minor in English, he became a social studies teacher at Scotland Neck, NC. He later completed his Masters degree and became the principal of an elementary school in Hobgood.

Mr. Williams' first novel, *First for Freedom* was originally written as a three-act play. The play was sponsored by the Halifax Historical Association and is presented each summer as an outdoor drama in Halifax, N.C. He also wrote the words and music for the drama.

Printed in the United States
1434500005B/178-192